The Journey to Cultural Championship:
Creating a passionate, driven, and high-performing team

Originally printed in:
Morrisville, North Carolina, USA

Written by:
Thomas MacIntosh & Matthias Jang
2019

Edited by Danielle Harder

First Printing: 2019

Published by:

Predictive Success Corporation
310 Byron Street South
Whitby, Ontario, Canada L1N 4P8

Predictive Success America Inc.
266 Elmwood Ave Suite 931
Buffalo, NY 14222

www.predictivesuccess.com

Table of Contents

Part 1: New Insights for the Conscience Manager

Part 2: Building a Company Culture

Part 3: Creating Generational Champions

Part 4: The Interviews

Acknowledgements

To the amazing team at Predictive Success for their support and expertise. We loved blogging about the use of predictive analytics to grow people and companies.

- Thomas and Matthias
July, 2019
Toronto, Canada

Dedication

To Mike Zani, CEO of The Predictive Index, and Daniel Muzquiz, Chair, who are both cultural champion leaders and creators of a talent-optimized company.

To Mom, Dad, Jack and Pete. – Thomas

To Mom and Dad, who have supported me through thick and thin. - Matthias

Foreword

I've been at all levels of organizations.

One summer I worked in my father's steel brush plant in Almonte, Ontario. I was the student, disengaged with my work and counting down the seconds until 5 p.m. when I could head off to hockey.

As an Enterprise Global Manager, Financial Services at Microsoft, however, I never even looked at the clock, much less knew when 5 p.m. hit. There, I worked with a great team led by an amazing boss—who I was even quoted as saying I would have "taken two bullets for."

Now this isn't to say there was something wrong with my father's business. In fact, his employees were engaged in their work, performed well, and grew the company profit year over year. However, in my case, I was in the wrong job and hated it and performed marginally.

Being in a job you actually love is nirvana for most. You may already know who these people are in your organization. They come in engaged in their job, have new ideas, create value for the business, and if the management team can identify this, are generally promoted through the hierarchal ranks of the company. This was me at Microsoft, completely engaged in what I was doing. Why? The job fit my personality and my boss set me up in the perfect job model to match it.

Today, I've come full circle in my business career. I was the part-time student, the full-time employee, and now an executive with people reports.

At Predictive Success, we work with companies to make sure they are hiring candidates who, at the microscopic level of their DNA, are naturally suited for the job. As a byproduct of this work, we spend a lot of time reading and conducting research on the Canadian workplace. We speak with business leaders every day, hear their success stories and their pain points. In almost every case the issues root back to not having the right people in the right jobs. Managers go by resumes and "gut-feeling"—hoping and praying their pick is the cultural champion I mentioned earlier.

It's not always even making the *wrong* pick, sometimes it's an issue of simply *finding* talent. According to a study from Boston-based software firm The Predictive Index, the top issue CEOs named in their business?

Finding the right talent.

This outranked "building better operational processes," "building a solid business strategy," and "developing new products and services." This is 100% consistent with what we have seen in our research.

Companies that can build a cultural championship, hire the right talent, and nurture it to become the future leaders of the company far outpace their stagnant counterparts.

At Predictive Success, we look for this every day, and we believe we have done a great job of building a cultural championship. We grow each year, are a three-time Profit 500 award-winner, and best of all, our team works incredibly hard in the office every day with a smile on their face. You can feel it, it's an energy that after 30 years in business I can recognize immediately. A team full of cultural champions.

When we were approached about this book, it was sort of a coincidental moment. Two of my youngest employees wanted to do something 19- and 20-year-old kids generally don't even think about. They wanted to go beyond what earned them money – to work on a project on the weekend, and develop something that would grow the company, but more importantly, grow themselves. The ironic part was that the book was going to be written about creating a cultural championship in the 21st century, and by the exact nature of what they did, these two were adding to the cultural championship we have built here.

In this book is a culmination of research, blog entries, interviews with industry experts, and more. I hope the findings and comments give you pause to evaluate your own company, your atmosphere, and whether you are creating culture champions within your organization.

If you would like to know more about what we do, how we grow culture in a business, and manage people to perform, I'd love to speak with you. Helping companies grow by leveraging their people strategy is what engages me in our work and helps me to add to the cultural championship we have today.

- **David Lahey**, MBA
  Founder and President, Predictive Success Corporation
  Bestselling Author, *Predicting Success: Evidence-Based Strategies to Hire the Right People and Build the Best Team* (Wiley, USA, 2015)

  July 2019

Introduction

We have all been there. That one hockey team you played on growing up, that one department you worked with, or the team you led. That one group of people who seemed to fit together perfectly, each controlling a moving part that—when combined—created magic.

This is a sort of bliss you don't get in every team. Often, there are people in a group who seem to swim like a salmon: upstream and against the flow. They mess with the rhythm of the others and often end up blocking the group's engagement and performance.

It's not always this person's fault. Sometimes we are thrust into a role we don't suit. We can try our best to make it work, bending our behaviour to the position, grinding through the tasks that make us groan, or putting on our mask and playing pretend. But at the end of the day we breathe a sigh of relief and resort back to our true self.

This type of person is what David Lahey, Founder and President of Predictive Success calls, "chair-spinners." These are the people who wait for the clock to strike 5 p.m. and run out the door so fast that by 5:05 their chair is still going around in circles. These are the employees who are not in the right job and see no value in building the company. Who wants to be engaged in something that doesn't engage them?

These individuals will never stay late to push through that big project, don't go to sleep at night with ideas for tomorrow, and probably won't try to engage that new employee in their work.

On the other end of the spectrum are the cultural champions.

We all know someone in our team like this. They come in each morning and make an extra effort on their work because the success of the business matters to them, not the number on the pay stub. They have ideas, grow with the company, and provide guidance to all the freshly hired employees who walk through the door.

Generally, companies are made up of a mixture of both types of people. By chance, the HR department hires a mixture of culture champions and chair spinners. The two groups interact every day, the champions putting the pedal to the metal while the chair spinners hammer on the break. Eventually, what emerges is a sort of "two steps forward, one step back."

The best companies in the world create cultural championships, businesses made of only those types of people. All feet are slamming the pedal through the floor, no brake lights in sight.

A million questions arise when talking about building a "cultural championship."

Is this even possible? How do you identify potential cultural champions in the hiring process? How do you nurture cultural champions? How do you adapt your cultural approach to fit the various generations in your organization.

A road map to this utopia is the goal of this book. By addressing several daunting questions, we hope to give the 21st century manager the ideas, stories, and data-backed insights into the modern workplace, with key action items for setting their organization on the road to cultural success.

Building a Cultural Championship: Creating a passionate, driven, and high-performing team is the executive's guide to the future of the workplace, from the minds of those who will soon be the largest generation in it.

- **Thomas MacIntosh and Matthias Jang**

Part 1: New Insights for the Conscience Manager

Chapter 1
AI and The Future of Consulting

"AI will either be the best or worst thing to ever happen to humanity." – **Stephen Hawking**

Becoming a consultant is a badge of honour for those in the corporate world. It signifies years of experience, education, and success, a sort of rite of passage to bestow your years of experience on hungry up and commers. However, in 2019, that industry is under threat.

The consulting model produces several issues. First, it's quite labour intensive, as the consultant is essentially the product. Second, it's a billable, time-based model. Every hour, no matter how productive it is, will be billed to a client. Finally, the consulting firm is only as good, and can only last as long, as it's consultants. If a firm has a few consultants that have great experience in the automotive industry, the firm can only be a leader in that field if those partners are still working at the firm. Unless they can find someone with the same specialized knowledge to fill their spot once the expert leaves.

What's more, many CEOs feel their talent strategy is the true backbone of their success, not business strategy under a consultant. One survey of 156 CEOs from The Predictive Index had 30% rank their talent strategy as their top priority, with a focus on business strategy taking the passenger seat.

This idea makes sense. If the human is the driver and backbone of your business, everything else doesn't work unless the people side works.

So how will management consulting firms need to shift in order to take advantage of the next wave of consulting? Artificial intelligence and software. The programs are flexible, customizable, scalable, and never leave the company. They can also better adapt to management consulting trends because of its data-driven approach.

When looking to make a decision about that same automotive industry, AI or software programs could make choices based on 100 terabytes of the most up-to-date industry information available. This allows companies to increase decision time, consider more data, and make a more informed choice. The best part is that the programs get smarter with each use.

Take, for example, DataRPM, an AI program that gets to know a machine and can predict future breakdowns, increasing asset life, long-term planning, and operational efficiency. This planning, often outsourced to knowledge experts in the automotive industry, can now be made using real-time data and analytics. This saves time and decreases consulting expenses.

AI and other software are the future of consulting. Although the human touch will always be required, the data-driven approach allows companies to use a wider variety of data to make more informed choices, allowing them to respond better to market trends for a fraction of the cost.

Sources
i ii iii iv

Chapter 2
Finding a Competitive Advantage in the Era of Data-Overload

"Not finance. Not strategy. Not technology. It is teamwork that remains the ultimate competitive advantage, both because it is so powerful and so rare."
- Patrick Lencioni
Author

In 1899, the Winton Motor Carriage Company created the world's first transport vehicle. The first companies to use this new machine had a competitive advantage over other companies that still used trains to transport their goods, as a truck could reach remote rural areas the trains couldn't.

When the Xerox Alto came out in 1973, it allowed users to employ a user interface that was more efficient than the typical computer. The first companies to implement these new interfaces saw a spike in productivity among employees, giving them a competitive advantage over companies that couldn't afford to make the switch.

So now, in the age of cost-efficient technology and data-overload, how do you develop and keep a competitive advantage? By going back to the one thing that never changes: humans.

By employing the right people in the right position, companies can create a strong backbone to grow, reduce turnover, and save money that can be invested in future development instead. By using talent optimization strategies to find the right fit, companies can ensure they are employing people who will keep them ahead of the curve, even as technology and markets continue to change. Investments in hiring the right employees create a trickle-down effect, as saved hiring costs can be reinvested to promote growth.

Hiring using data has become the go-to method for ensuring companies are hiring top-tier talent. Data-backed measurements allow companies to use key metrics for hiring, allowing them to see behavioural traits in relation to a specific job. How does this materialize as a competitive advantage in different industries? For two different industries, investments in talent optimization directly translated into decreased turnover, increased revenue, and business growth.

Restaurant and Food Service
Some restaurants see three in four staff members depart annually. With such a high turnover rate, restaurant owners must think critically about their hiring decisions.

Hiring and firing costs can be one of the biggest annual expenses for the over 60,000 restaurant owners in Canada, and more than 1 million owners in the U.S. In fact, Cornell University calculated that the average loss of a restaurant employee can cost $5,864 USD. Roughly one-half of departures from these jobs come from employees who aren't suited to the work they are doing.

For a restaurant with 40 employees, this could mean a loss of $171,228.80 per year. By using a data-backed hiring process, with a behavioural assessment to asses candidate fit, this same restaurant could see turnover reduce by up to 29%, which translates into just over $68,000 in retained income, all from hiring the right people. This $68,000 could allow for major renovations, new investments in efficient technology, or increased marketing spending—all of which represent other areas of competitive advantage.

Technology and Software

In the hyper-competitive job market, the right hires can make or break a technology company.

According to *Canadian HR Reporter*, the technology and software industry has one of the highest turnover rates in Canada at 16.9%. With a demand for top talent and low barriers to entry in the sector, new companies are continually popping up, increasing the demand for top developers, engineers, and business development executives. In the U.S., it takes an average of 23.8 days to replace a vacant seat. This means lost productivity and output for a company, a factor that can be disastrous in a hyper-competitive marketplace where productivity is sometimes the sole determinant of success.

Ironically, it seems that the best way to create a competitive advantage in the year of constant change is to go back to the one part of a business that has never changed.

People.

Sources
v vi vii viii

Chapter 3
Hiring on the "Skinny Resume ®"

The person born with a talent they are meant to use will find their greatest happiness in using it.
– Johann Wolfgang van Goethe
Writer

As a student, there is one word you hear quite often, possibly more than any other word throughout your educational career: resume. From the time you nervously step foot through the doors of high school, to the day you hang your degree or diploma on the wall, teachers, administrators, and leaders of all sorts pitch their class, degree, or program as "something that looks good on your resume."

They pitch this for good reason. Some employers spend just 11 seconds looking at a resume, so the more experience, relevant skills, and education you can cram in, the better chance you have of getting hired. For your employer, the more you see on a resume, the better chance that candidate will be hanging on your "Employee of the Month" wall next month.

Right?

The issues with this method of hiring could fill a book, but the main three reasons boil down to:

1. According to Inc.com, 85% of people have lied or embellished a resume. This is invisible to the hiring manager during the interview but will be evident when they show up for the first day of work.

2. Experience does not mean someone is naturally fit for a job.

3. And the most important of all, some great candidates can't break into the market, and thus can't get hired on a "resume-only" model, no matter how great they *could* be.

This last one is key. With 5.75 million jobs currently open in Canada, why is it that companies can't seem to find qualified employees, while young adults can't seem to find work? The gap exists as an invisible barrier between employer and candidate, a barrier of experience that could provide the employer with the confidence they need to be confident in hiring the incredible candidate they have before them. That's essentially all resumes provide to employers: confidence that someone can do a job.

In 2019, however, there is a better way to provide hiring staff the confidence they need to have in a candidate's ability to do what they say they can do. Behavioural assessments provide insights into someone's genetic capabilities, allowing employers to determine a candidate fit for a role, regardless of their experience. On average, companies who use behavioural assessments see a decrease of up to 29% when it comes to bad hires.

For example, take a programming student applying to a software firm right out of school. Maybe they have never worked on enterprise software as a job, however, they have a natural orientation towards being detail-oriented and patient. Education? Check. Natural abilities that fit with the job? Check. Hiring on the skinny resume.

The major argument an employer may make to this is, "yes they may naturally be good for a job, but there are industry skills they need to have." This is the easier part to teach. When you are confident you have hired someone, who is naturally fit for their job, you can teach the industry skills. You can't teach detail orientation or patience. Ask any manager, teacher, or parent about a child who is naturally gifted in a discipline, they have talents you can't teach.

Hiring based on resumes opens managers up to being duped by those who interview well or those who lie and embellish their resume. Behavioural assessments allow companies to see past the resume and have a sense of trust in the abilities of their hire, no matter their experience. This allows companies to craft the ideal candidate, whose industry-specific skills can be built up in the job.

Hire on the DNA, build the resume yourself.

Sources
ix x xi xii

Chapter 4
Social Recruiting: A New Hiring Tool

"Social media is not a media. The key is to listen, engage, and build relationships." – **David Alston**
Entrepreneur and Public
Speaker

From medicine to technology, many facets of society have advanced dramatically in recent decades—and recruiting is no exception. Long gone are the days of newspaper job listings and casual word-of-mouth. The workplace is becoming increasingly competitive and attracting top talent now requires more intentional recruitment strategies. One strategy that allows firms to effectively target candidates with key qualifications is called social recruitment. With the advent and increasingly universal use of social media, it is essential that hiring managers adapt to the changing labour market by adding social recruiting to their arsenal of recruitment tools.

What is social recruitment?

As a new generation of digital natives enters the workforce, businesses should view social media as a platform for candidate discovery and evaluation. Social recruiting is a powerful tool that integrates the use of popular social media platforms—such as LinkedIn, Facebook, and Twitter—as a means of hiring potential employees. By listing job openings on social media, firms cannot only benefit from widespread exposure and increased accessibility but can also decrease recruitment expenses and streamline the hiring process.

Why consider social recruitment?

Millennials are using social media to look for jobs.

According to the Aberdeen Group, 73% of Millennials found their last position through a social media platform, making them one of the principal causes of social recruitment practices. For firms wanting to target one of the largest and fastest growing workforces, a strong social media presence is vital. Additionally, people spend a lot of time on social media. If global media consumption continues on the same path, the average person will have spent the equivalent of 5 years on social media platforms during their lifetime.

Candidates who find your job through social media might be a better fit.

At least 58% of U.S. consumers use social media to follow brands they enjoy. Employee candidates who apply to a firm's job posting through social media were only able to find that job posting either because they purposefully sought out the firm or because they expressed interest in relevant and related business functions. This means that these types of candidates have already shown an intrinsic interest in the firms to which they are applying.

Social recruiting harnesses the power of employee connections.

Social referral programs are an effective and streamlined way of reaching qualified candidates. Word-of-mouth and employee referrals have a high success rate—65% of people would consider a new job opportunity if it were personally referred to them, according to Monster.

The best enabler of this sort of behaviour is through social media. For instance, Nielsen reports that 92% of people prefer recommendations from friends and family over any marketing or promotional material.

As an increasing number of businesses innovate their recruitment strategies, social recruiting is certain to be at the forefront of this movement. Social recruitment may now seem like an effective hiring strategy, but it is important to remember that without careful, methodical implementation, all potential benefits can be lost.

Additionally, social recruiting does not have to be used in isolation of other recruitment strategies. By combining this tool with traditional recruitment efforts, firms can maximize their chances of attracting the most qualified job applicants.

A wide net catches more fish, especially when the fish were already interested in the net in the first place.

Sources
xiii xiv xv xvi xvii

Chapter 5
Why Data is the New Corporate Superpower

"Data is the new oil."
— **Clive Humby**
Author

Data analytics have taken the recruitment process by storm. Modern companies use data at every stage of the talent lifecycle to strengthen the decision-making process—and companies that don't are getting left behind. In recent years, data analytics, sometimes called predictive analytics, have been in the limelight of the HR news world.

We hear about it all the time in the development of artificial intelligence, in the application of cognitive and behavioural aptitude tests and so on. But how exactly is data employed in the practical setting? How often is it used and why is it used? This question can be explored by examining how successful corporations are integrating data in extraordinary ways.

According to a LinkedIn Talent Solutions Report, 69% of talent professionals believe using data can elevate their careers. This is why Nielsen Holdings, a global information, data and measurement company, believes it can use people data to reduce turnover.

By analyzing attrition data from the past five years, Nielsen's People Analytics teams discovered that employees with a change in job responsibilities due to promotion or lateral movement within the past two years were much less likely to leave. Acting on this information, Nielsen's leadership focused on presenting high-performers and 'at-risk' employees with ample opportunity to pursue new positions internally. This emphasis on presenting the opportunity for corporate movement helped Nielsen realize a 5-10% increase in annual retention of their at-risk employees.

Every year, JetBlue Airways evaluates over 125,000 applicants for flight attendant roles by using psychological assessments, structured interviews, video interviews and work samples against eight target traits. Being "nice" was one of those traits. It made intuitive sense to JetBlue leadership that flight attendants should be kind to passengers.

However, by analyzing customer feedback data, it was brought to JetBlue's attention that "nice" took a strong backseat to "helpful." Customers far preferred a helpful attendant to one that was nice, allowing JetBlue to cater its employees' traits to the needs of its customers. In fact, being helpful can balance out the effect of a flight attendant who is not nice. The results of this small change to recruitment criteria were astonishing. A rise in employee engagement and retention meant that employee absences decreased by 12%, an important factor in preventing delays and cancellations of flights. JetBlue also reported a small increase in customer satisfaction, a win-win situation for all.

The employee recruiting process has come a long way since the early days of gut-based decision making. As more companies use data analytics to their advantage, hiring is becoming increasingly scientific. However, that does not mean those who do not have a propensity for numbers should be intimidated. At the end of the day, behind all the numbers and the spreadsheets, recruiting talent is still about the people.

It is people who drive the hiring process, not numbers. But data-driven recruiting, if used the right way, can amplify the results of even the most robust recruiting processes. By taking the generated data and asking relevant questions based on the needs of the business, talent teams can push their hiring systems to a new standard. Managers should not be afraid of implementing data analytics into their businesses. Data is becoming a top tool, affecting the way thousands of businesses hire employees. This is because data drives results in a concrete, factual manner.

Although there are a million factors (or so it seems) in every business decision, data presents a backbone for managers and executives to use when they need to back up decisions—a safety net for the modern decision-maker.

Sources

xviii

Chapter 6
Pre-Employment Screening is Becoming Increasingly Important

"Far and away the best prize that life offers is the chance to work hard at work worth doing."
– Theodore Roosevelt,
U.S. President 1901 - 1909

According to the U.S. Labor Department, the unemployment rate in America dropped to an astounding 3.6% in April of 2019, the lowest it has been since 1969. Job market growth has also been strong north of the border, according to Statistics Canada, which announced that Canada's total employment growth rate was roughly 2.3% year-over-year. Canada has also seen a downward trend in national unemployment, sitting around 5.7%, down about 1.3% from 2016.

Strong economic growth across both countries has been conducive to a thriving job market. But as the job market grows, so does the pool of job applicants. An increasing number of applicants may seem inherently spectacular—more applicants, more talent.

The downside to a growing candidate pool, however, is that without a proper screening process companies also increase the chances of making a poor and costly hiring decision. According to a 2017 SHRM survey, making the wrong hiring decision can cost upwards of $5,000 USD for an organization.

Given the dramatic growth of the North American workforce in recent years, employers can no longer rely solely on candidate interviews to make reliable choices about employee hiring. Pre-employment tests can curtail these obstacles. Administering behavioural and cognitive aptitude tests, for example, can shed deeper insights on a candidate's potential, allowing companies to make better informed, and more accurate hiring decisions.

Additionally, an employment pre-screening process can reveal critical information about a candidate that would otherwise have been inaccessible to a company prior to employment. This can include details such as employment verification, substance abuse habits, credit history, driving records, and criminal convictions—all relevant details associated with employee performance.

The most immediate benefit of implementing pre-employment tests is a general improvement in the quality of applicants. According to a 2017 employment screening benchmark report by Inc.com, 85% of resumes contain falsified or exaggerated information. Announcing that pre-employment testing will be part of the job application process is likely to deter dishonest candidates from even submitting an application. At a minimum, it will increase the likelihood of honest representation in the interview.

Another fundamental advantage to pre-employment tests is that they are cost-efficient investments for the long run. In addition to avoiding the cost of lost productivity and employee turnover, the process of screening job applicants can prevent costs that would otherwise have been irreparable. Serious employee misconduct such as fraud or theft of company confidential information can permanently damage a company's brand and goodwill. Instead of hoping that employees will always behave in good faith, organizations can ensure their longevity by investing in early screening measures, so as to prevent undesired behaviour in the first place.

Implementing a process to screen potential job applicants also fulfills a company's legal responsibilities. For example, hiring somebody for a truck driving position without running the necessary background checks can lead to a dangerous situation. If the truck driver were to cause an accident due to the influence of alcohol, authorities would look to the employer to see if it had fulfilled its due diligence.

If it is revealed that the truck driver has a history of impaired driving, the employer could be held liable for the accident. Failure to process the necessary background checks on an employee is called negligent hiring, a legal theory in which an employer can be held responsible for an accident caused by an employee if it is determined that a screening should have been performed was not. To protect a company's reputation and image, it is better to cover all required bases.

Pre-screening methods such as aptitude and personality tests also provide interviewers with a more complete picture of a particular applicant. The interview process has become so standardized that it is becoming increasingly difficult to know what a candidate would be like in a working environment.

By administering behavioural and cognitive assessments to job candidates, employers can get a more accurate sense of the person they are interviewing and if they would fit the company dynamic. Regardless of how polished someone may appear in an interview, screening measures can offer a glimpse at their true abilities.

Data: the cure to the "hiring veil."

Sources
xix xx xxi xxii xxiii xxiv xxv

Chapter 7

How Expensive is the Wrong Hire—and How Can Businesses Avoid It?

"If you make a hiring mistake, make the change quickly. Don't ignore problems. Don't assume it will get better."
— Ziad K. Abdelnour
Author, *Economic Warfare: Secrets of Wealth Creation in the Age of Welfare Politics*

There is one form of risk that transcends income levels, industries, and experience, while simultaneously affecting every business, sports team, club, or academic program in the same way.

That factor is people.

A bad coach can lose a game, a poorly chosen club president can lead an organization down the wrong path, and a 'mis-hire' can be a toxic addition to what might otherwise be a fantastic business culture. We can all identify a time in our lives when we worked with or managed a toxic employee. This person slows productivity, creates tension in the office, and isn't a right fit for the job. As a manager of one of these employees, you understand all too well the effect this employee is having on others but what many managers don't measure—or don't know how to measure—is the dollar-for-dollar cost of this employee.

A major SHRM research study in 2017 attempted to quantify this cost to a business, with results that may make managers rethink their recruitment process.

The Research

SHRM studied 488 firms that were in the process of hiring low to mid-level employees, as well as 247 firms hiring an executive-level employee. The firms used a variety of processes to recruit candidates, with the top methods being employee referrals (90%), job boards (71%), and social media (61%) for mid-level candidates. For the executive search, most firms used networking events (61%) or executive search firms (49%).

From there, SHRM looked at how the firms assessed candidates. Perhaps not surprisingly, roughly 75% of firms used references to get an idea of a candidate's true behaviour, while just over two-thirds used a one-on-one meeting with the candidate. Only about 25% of firms used a behavioural assessment to evaluate a potential employee, while an even fewer (17%) used cognitive assessment. So, with traditional methods of hiring still prevailing as the "go-to" how did these employees fare and what was the cost?

SHRM was able to average out the cost of a hire for mid-level and executive-level employees. The numbers were staggering.

The average cost for a low to mid-level hire, something most companies do on an almost continual basis: $4,425. One in four of these companies paid more than $4,650 per hire.

The cost of an executive hire was even greater. The average firm spent $14,936, with one in four firms spending more than $18,000 per hire.
For firms that hire even two low to mid-level employees per year, this could mean close to $10,000 in hiring expenses, while hiring two executives could cost close to $30,000. This represents a major capital expenditure for some businesses, and a mis-hire could mean lost abilities to pursue growth-related initiatives.

SHRM followed up with the firms to see what happened with the employees and the length of their hiring process. For 864 separate hires, the average time to fill a job was 36 days. For 602 of those hires, 26% were gone within a year.

Translation: for the average firm hiring 10 people a year, this means $11,505 wasted on hiring the wrong person. To go further, that number doesn't consider lost productivity during the 36 days, as well as the stress to the rest of the team.

Beyond the monetary value, these mis-hires influence company culture, often hampering the productivity of other employees (something we tackle later in this book).

Much the same as the infamous Mastercard commercial: this company culture is priceless.

Sources
xxvi xxvii

Chapter 8
Marketing to Generation Z

"Brands targeting Gen Z need to look beyond the confines of traditional segmentation, the ultimate priority always has to be on alignment that helps us cultivate relationships with youth culture - not just organize it." - **Gregg L. Witt**
Author, *The Gen Z Frequency: How Brands Tune in and Build Credibility*

Marketing to Generation Z generally conjures up only one phrase: social media. This chapter could probably be the entire book: However, that would make it just another one of the 56.2 million 'Social Media and Generation Z' hits on Google.

It is impossible, however, to just ignore social media when talking about marketing to Generation Z. The words are synonymous. So, what does social media mean to those born after 1996, without just saying "everything"?

As it turns out, social media is merely the symptom of Generation Z. Two researchers, Kaylene Williams of California State University, and Robert Page of Southern Connecticut State University, penned an article in The Journal of Behavioral Studies in Business on the topic of "Marketing to Generations." Interestingly, Williams' and Page's conclusions after studying Generation Z describe the age group with words many would deem completely contradictory to that of social media. Generation Z values authenticity and "realness." If you have made the conclusion that Generation Z = social media, and this statement says Generation Z = realness, then that means social media = realness.
Right?

Statistics are not needed to prove that most people wouldn't agree with the former statement. If you still feel you need some evidence, watch AJR's music video entitled "Pretender." It's a very accurate representation of current social media trends.

So, backing up, how did Williams and Page come to this conclusion?

Well, imagine you're born in 1999 (a great year to be born if we do say so ourselves). At the time of publishing this book, you are 19 or 20-years-old. That means Facebook, which launched on February 4, 2004, became the world superpower it is today right around the time you were starting school. We never needed older generations to explain to us that Facebook contained fake content; we saw it every day. We never needed to be told that there was bullying online, we saw it. For our generation, we were watching the catastrophe happen before the adults started ringing the warning bells.

We can vividly remember seeing people's pictures on Facebook and thinking, "That's not at all what they look like in person." It wasn't something that phased us. It was just a fact that we knew and it changed how we interacted online. When we were old enough to notice marketing efforts, this skepticism—derived from years of exposure to content we knew was fake—carried with us.

As a generation, we demand that brands be transparent and real. TOMS® Shoes are a great example of a company that took advantage of this notion. The company's entire marketing strategy was centered around the connection between its sales and its charity work. The One for One® campaign pledged that for every pair of TOMS® shoes sold, the company would donate a pair to someone who needs them. To date, the company has donated 86 million pairs, a pretty solid record.

The company's brilliance was in the simplicity of the campaign. It's easy to stay transparent when your promise is so simple. Easy to understand for all involved. TOMS® has extended the campaign to include restoring sight in patients in developing nations (tied one for one to the number of pairs of glasses they sell), access to clean drinking water, (tied one for one to the number of bags of coffee they sell), and safe birthing practices (tied one for one to the number of bags they sell).

The brilliance of TOMS® lies in its distinct branding as a socially conscience company with tiebacks to individual products. By making certain products support certain efforts, TOMS® sub-consciously gives consumers active participation in deciding what they support. This invitation to participate in charity work backs the consumer's original decision to buy, and can help to push them over the hump towards a sale.

Managers and business owners alike could benefit from finding their "niche charity" in 2019, all while giving back. Not only will this build a company's sales but also build the company's internal culture of teamwork as employees work together to support social efforts.

Sources
xxviii xxix xxx

Chapter 9
New Trends and Historic Industries

"Technology's always changing. There was a time where oil painting was a new technology. That changed painting."
– Joe Bradley
Artist

One of the greatest traits a current Gen X or Baby Boomer manager can have is a willingness to embrace new trends and technology. Believe it or not, there are manufacturing companies with successful social media profiles and factories with podcasts. On the technology side, there are solutions to almost any problem. Need to edit your PDF? There's a company for that. Need to automate your Twitter account? There's a company for that. Want to find a way to have a conference call without buying conference call equipment? Yep, there's a company for that too.

But how do you, as a manager, apply technology and trends to successful industries that were around longer than computers?

The classic response to a tech-suggestion when speaking with someone in an "old" industry is "my industry can't use that, we are a (blank), not a tech start-up." It's an almost knee-jerk reaction. However, because of the abilities of the internet, technology is customizable and can even be an asset in industries that have been slow to adopt innovation.

Take a moving company, for example. A classic business since people have always moved houses, but not one that seems synonymous with social media. Who wants to see updates about a moving company? Flip the script a little and consider more than just the face of the business. Moving companies are synonymous with homes and people love to read about homes.

Also connected to the moving business is a home decoration, real estate, and landscaping. There is more content on these subjects available on the internet than any moving company could ever post to its Facebook account. Boom. A social media strategy (new solution) for a moving company (old industry).

Also consider a manufacturing company having a webinar series. Its management team would have more than enough experience to provide valuable insight on safety, purchasing, and supply chain management to young entrepreneurs who may also become clients. The company can use this new tool to educate those in their field, become knowledge experts in the eyes of their industry, while also drawing in new clients in the process.

How do you do this in your organization?

Think of your company as a golf hole with the green as your industry and the peripheral—the fairway—as area for new growth and innovative ideas. What topics that people talk about online sit on your fairway and can connect to your green?

Chapter 10
A Brief History of Predictive Analytics

"As data piles up, we have ourselves a genuine gold rush. But data isn't the gold. I repeat, data in its raw form is boring crud. The gold is what is discovered therein." –
Eric Siegel
Author, *Predictive Analytics: The Power to Predict Who Will Click, Buy, Lie, or Die*

Moore's law dictates that technology becomes two times faster, and half as expensive, every two years. This hypothesis has been substantiated by the rapid expansion in the realm of computer-processing abilities. A by-product of this advancement was predictive analytics models like regression and machine learning techniques. These predictive models changed our ability to process and accurately utilize large quantities of data.

Thus, it can be presumed that models such as the ones above must have come around a few years after the creation of the first computer in the late 1930s, when the smart people who designed the computer realized what it was capable of, right?

Well, although these advanced techniques are only about sixty years old, the concept of humans analyzing the past to predict future characteristics actually dates to the 17th century, which begins the first of five phases of predictive analytics.

Phase 1: Basic Analytics – The Lloyd Company

In 1689, predictive analytics was used by the Lloyd company to underwrite insurance for sea voyages. Using data, the company would accept the risk of sea voyages in return for a premium. Lloyd used data sets of past trips in order to evaluate the risk of these voyages and predict patterns of liability. Lloyds continues to use predictive models in all facets of their insurance underwriting, and the idea has become general-practice in the insurance industry.

Phase 2: Descriptive Phase – What Happened?

Fast-forward to the mid 20th century, just after the invention of the computer. The Description Phase linked the Lloyd Company idea of "what happened," with the modern computer, to create the basic models of linear programming and computational modeling. These models have become the driver of several business functions in almost every industry in the world.

Phase 3: The Diagnostic Phase – Why Did it Happen?

Into the mid-1970s, predictive analysis evolved to encompass the question of why something happened, instead of just what happened. This analysis looked for root-causes and was the backbone of several innovations that would improve business functions, including optimization and maximization. It was also during this period that the computers made large jumps in storage and processing capabilities, allowing functions to become that much more effective.

Phase 4: The Predictive Phase – What Will Happen?

The late 20th century and dawn of the 21st century saw the beginning of the predictive phase. The development of mathematical models that utilized weighting techniques to score data sets were programmed into analytical programs. This allowed the computer to make suggestions and predict outcomes based on a series of inputs.

Phase 5: The Cognitive Phase – Machine Learning and the Future

With continually increasing processing speeds, and innovations in programming, machine learning and artificial intelligence have created a climate that can allow computers to increase accuracy levels in predictive software without human intervention. These programs will be the future of almost anything we can conceive. Although the prospect of machine learning, and its ability to consistently improve a program's 'intelligence' can seem rather scary, the actual future of this phase will create benefits for safety, healthcare, and international markets.

Predictive analytics has evolved greatly since the days of the Lloyd Insurance Company, but the drive remains the same: to utilize data and patterns to decrease description cost, increase accuracy, and provide managers with the tools to make the right decision the first time.

Sources
xxxi xxxii

Chapter 11
What Separate the 'Good' and the 'Great"

"The true genius of a great manager is his or her ability to individualize. A great manager is one who understands how to trip each person's trigger."
— **Marcus Buckingham**
Author, *First, Break All the Rules*

A company's most valuable asset can be its people. For many businesses, its employees—the work they do and the passion they feel—can be the difference between success and failure.

Over the years, the value of a corporation's human capital has become increasingly acknowledged. It is why Google offers delicious, free meals and snacks in the office and why Airbnb provides its employees with an annual stipend of $2,000 to travel the world. Although extravagant employee perks are enticing, nothing can impact an employee's engagement, loyalty, and productivity like a great manager.

The findings from both Google's Project Oxygen and The Predictive Index's People Management Survey corroborate this sentiment. Time and time again, "people rely on their managers to make clear decisions and facilitate collaboration across teams" according to the internal researchers of Project Oxygen.

How to Become a Great Manager

It has been established that great managers are the key to a productive and effective workforce. But this begs two questions: How can we become great managers? How can we curate an environment in which personal growth, energy, and passion levels are on full throttle?

The answer to these questions can—at least, in part—be found in research conducted by Google's Project Oxygen and The Predictive Index's People Management Survey. The research from both these studies found that the difference between a good manager and a great manager can be boiled down to a few, nuanced traits.

Here is a list of some traits that all great managers share.

Being a strong decision maker.

A core component of being able to lead others. The ability to make clear, quick decisions on tough matters is a skill that 78% of great managers share, according to The Predictive Index's People Management Survey.

As our economy evolves, so do our needs in the workplace. Employees want to know that their managers are concerned with their well-being and success, more so than ever before. Managers need to make a conscious effort to let employees know they are valued. This can start by listening to what employees have to say, whether it be in the meeting room or in the coffee lounge.

Having a strong work ethic.

Lead by example. Old adages often hold some truth, and this one is no exception. Employees need a role model that they can respect. If the manager does not work hard, how can anyone expect any different from the employees?

A family-friend of mine who works as a Vice-President of a Toronto-area middle school embodies this practice. By showing patience and empathy with the kids, and actively working to improve their situation, he is a work ethic role model for the teachers around him. Because of this, many of the teachers working with him embody this work style, and make the school a better place.

Supporting career development.

Great managers will support their employees beyond the scope of the job. It is crucial that employees are treated as people and that they are recognized as having a purpose and goal with regards to professional development. It could be helpful to have a meaningful conversation with employees about their career aspirations and their employee performance. These kinds of conversations show empathy and concern for the employee's well-being, which in turn can help improve worker morale and energy.

Being honest.

Employees want to be recognized as hard-working individuals, not monotonous machines. To respect the work that they do for their organization, it is always important to be honest. This signals to employees that they are appreciated. This trait plays into how important it is to have meaningful, constructive conversations.

What to Take Away.

From the research findings above, great managers do more than just manage employees, in the traditional sense. Great managers can *personalize* the work of their employees. They are listeners, friends, and advocates. They care about the well-being and development of their employees, and they make sure their employees know that. So next meeting, it might be worthwhile to take a moment and engage with your employees on a personal level. Start a conversation and show employees how much you value their work.

Sources
xxxiii xxxiv

Part 2: Building a Cultural Championship

Chapter 12
Managing Gen Z and Building Company Culture

"If you are lucky enough to be someone's employer, you have a moral obligation to make sure people do look forward to coming to work in the morning."
– Howard Schultz
CEO, Starbucks

The words, 'manager' and 'future' invariably go hand in hand. For many managers, the first few words of their job title include something relating to the future. The job descriptions for 'Long-Term Projects Manager,' 'Hiring Manager,' and 'Sales Manager' all include some form of glass-ball seeking outlook. So, for any manager with even a little bit of prospective ability, a question that should arise is: How will Generation Z change my workplace?

The common response might be to move the office in the direction of the stereotypical technology start-up. Open-concept desks, an in-house coffee shop, and office gym passes. However, rather ironically, they are actually symptoms of what Generation Z truly cares about.

Company culture.

As the top end of Generation Z blows out the candles on their 23rd birthday cakes and frames their newly minted post-secondary credentials, managers need to start analyzing their own company culture. For Gen Z, a company's purpose, the people they work with, and the opportunities they provide for growth all matter more than the number on the paycheque. Unlike other generations, salary was rated third in terms of importance by a group of Generation Z employees, according to an International Federation of Accountants workplace study. Rainmaker Thinking elaborated on this research, interviewing 4,000 more Gen Z-ers.

The two top needs for this wave of workers? A supportive leadership team and positive work relationships. The least important, according to these same employees born after 1996, was salary.

But how do you build a company culture? It's not something tangible, like sales numbers or output quantities. The answer lies in data-analytics.

By using behavioural assessments and workplace analytics tools that measure the compatibility of individuals and teams, leaders can cut through unnecessary noise to find out how individuals will interact with each other and identify pain points.

As a leader, how do you analytically measure your team's internal culture?

Sources
xxxv xxxvi

Chapter 13
Taking Time Off Can Actually Mean More Productivity

"Life moves pretty fast. If you don't stop and look around once in a while, you could miss it."
– Ferris Beuller
Ferris Beuller's Day Off, 1986

These famous words require no explanation, as the man who uttered them, with his whimsical outlook on life, have become an eternal point of reference for those who seek to time to relax.

The concept of work-life and work-rest balance are perceived differently by companies around the world. Generally, a company's outlook on the topic is determined by its geography.

In China, the 996 rule dominates the corporate world. An employee is expected to work from 9 a.m. to 9 p.m., six days a week. The fact that Chinese law caps work weeks at 44 hours is regarded as more of a suggestion than a rule. Cheng Zheng, founder of the Chinese start-up DDD Online, blames the introduction of the 996 rule on foreign competition, stating it's a necessity to stay relevant.

Move your desk globe about 90 degrees west and land in Italy, where companies take a two-hour break from 11:30 a.m. to 1:30 p.m., in order to cook and nap at home, completely opposite of the Chinese attitude. Both a 72-hour work week and 2-hour lunch break seem foreign to those of us working in the North American corporate world. However, there is a growing trend toward workplace relaxation here at home as well.

By working longer hours Monday through Thursday, employees are encouraged by some firms to follow in the footsteps of Mr. Bueller, and not report in on Fridays. The results of this method? Some companies have found a 10% retention rate increase where others increased productivity across the board.

Now, this method isn't feasible for all types of businesses. Some, by virtue of their industry, need to be in the office all week. However, there are still other ways to gain some of these same "work hard, relax hard" benefits.

Stimulating Creative Thinking Outside the Office

Predictive Success, for example, takes one summer day off each year to enjoy a baseball game, great food, and time together as a team outside the office. Fittingly dubbed "Ferris Bueller's Day Off" the day is something to look forward to as a team and a time to talk about non-work topics, which eventually circles back around to some creative thinking about the exact opposite.

Sometimes a team's problems can be solved by not trying to solve them. Giving time away from the desk can sometimes be more beneficial than being having people in them.

Sources
xxxvii xxxviii

Chapter 14
Implementing Social Recruiting

"Social media is not a media. The key is to listen, engage, and build relationships"
- **David Alston**

It may seem as if a social recruiting strategy is as simple as posting a job on Facebook, Twitter, and LinkedIn. But there is more to the process than that. The process of implementing a social recruiting strategy can be broken into three broad steps: Setting goals, choosing platforms, involving employee advocates.

Step 1: Setting Your Goals

As with any company initiative, it is important to set goals and key performance indicators. This allows managers to objectively identify progress and success when it happens. To begin, firms should consider a few things: what kinds of platforms to use, what kinds of jobs to post, and what kinds of candidates to attract. From the dozens of social media platforms available, it can be enticing to target audiences on every single one of those sites, but that strategy can lead to ineffective results with no real target audience.

Typically, there are slight nuances among the ways that companies engage with potential recruits depending on the social media platform. Below are just a few examples.

On Facebook: Companies can monitor candidates to get a glimpse into how they present themselves to friends, family, and strangers.

On Twitter: A conversational platform, Twitter can be used to chat with candidates or learn more about their interests and values—great for determining company fit.

On LinkedIn: A classic, LinkedIn can be used to gauge a candidate's professional experience—useful in determining whether a candidate is qualified for the position.

On Instagram: Firms can understand what the candidate likes to do in his or her spare time or what passions they have outside of work.

Step 2: Choosing the Right Platform

At times, finding qualified candidates can seem like searching for a needle in a haystack, which is why it is important for recruiters to use the appropriate platform given the role they are trying to fill. LinkedIn and Twitter may seem like the most obvious choices, but that is not always the case. For example, consider two job openings. One is for a graphic designer, the other is for a salesperson. The graphic designer may elect to spend more time on visual social media such as Instagram or Pinterest. The salesperson, however, may be more active on traditional platforms such as LinkedIn or Twitter.

By carefully considering the nature of the position they are trying to fill, recruiters can frame their social media recruiting strategies around where the best candidates are likely to spend the most time. Each platform will require a slightly different approach when recruiting. Twitter recruiters

will want to utilize hashtags and concise job descriptions in order to maximize visibility. Facebook recruiters may want to consider joining career
groups or job pages to find the best talent.

Step 3: Involve Employee Advocates

What is unique about a social recruiting strategy is that it is social. This
means that recruiters should leverage the power of connection with the
network they already have. Just by sharing job listings, company employees can exponentially improve a firm's chances of attracting a top-quality
candidate.

According to a study by Smarp, the average employee advocate has 400
LinkedIn contacts, 420 Facebook friends, and 360 Twitter followers. Additionally, the content shared by employees has an 8x higher engagement
rate than content shared by company profiles.

With over 98% of professionals using at least one social media site, recruiting managers have the potential to unlock a huge network of
exposure—one that is as close to home as possible. Potential candidates
want proof that current employees enjoy working for the firm. First-hand
testimonials from employee advocates can have huge, positive impacts on
a firm's recruiting strategy.

Firms that consistently attract top-tier talent almost always have some
form of a social recruiting strategy. But following the recruiting process is
the selection process—an entirely different challenge.

How does this contribute to culture?

By utilizing the expansive social networks at a manager's disposal, he or
she can search a large network of those who possess traits and experience
that will guide the company's future culture.

By hiring a candidate who has interacted with the brand online, companies
can ensure they are hiring passionate individuals. This passion is part of

the reason these individuals will show up to work, eager to push the company to new heights.

This is what culture is all about. When passionate employees are present, they inflict passion on those around them and are more likely to engage in and push new company initiatives that snowball as passion for others.

What are the tangible aspects of a passionate employee? According to Refresh Leadership, this can materialize as a number of traits.

First, passionate workers are focused. This is basic business, someone who enjoys what they do will continue to push for the prize.

Second, they are competitive. Watch the Olympics for ten minutes and watch a sprint for the finish. The raw perseverance and grit at that point is a direct passion = competitiveness equation.

Finally, perseverance isn't affected by failure. This means the business can make missteps without losing key players and having to completely rebuild.

Next time you go to hire, look for the user interacting with your brand every day. Maybe they have something to offer?

Sources
xxxix

Chapter 15
Using Analytics Instead of Your, "Gut."

"Without big data, you can't see or hear and are in the middle of a freeway."
– Geoffrey Moore
American Organizational Theorist

We have all heard it before: people judge you within seven seconds of meeting you. It's the reason we buy new dress clothes for job interviews and spend time making sure there is nothing on our face before we walk in the door for our first day of a new job.

However, this rule doesn't apply only to people. Try watching a show like *Dragon's Den* or *Shark Tank*, and not evaluating someone's business pitch right after they give their ask. A large share of this is trustworthiness. It's embedded in us as humans. We immediately evaluate "fight or flight."

Before predictive analytics, executives and those evaluating business ventures, partners, or job-candidates, had to rely on a gut feeling. This was the Descriptive Phase. As humans, we looked at what happened and used that to predict the future. "This candidate made their company $200,000 last year. If we hire them, we should expect something similar."

As analytics developed, we came into the Diagnostic Phase, where we looked at why something happened. "This business was able to diversify its risk against market downturns. *Why?* They used call options." Instead of just looking at what happened, we investigated to find out why it happened. However, we still used our gut to make a call. There was nothing to help us back up decisions we made on that understanding.

As we entered the Predictive Phase, where companies could use data to not only analyze past results but predict future results, we could base our decisions solidly in data. Every move we make can be made considering all available data on the Internet and beyond, provided you can access it.

So, why aren't all businesses implementing analytics in their business ASAP and what is happening to those that are?

About 65% of businesses in North America leverage some form of descriptive analytics, but only 30% of those same businesses are leveraging predictive analytics. Even further, just 18% of these companies feel they are seeing a positive ROI on their analytics investment.

The answer lies in a couple of areas but can be generalized by a few issues: poor data quality, an inability to describe the tangible benefits of analytics, and inadequate analyst training, in order to understand and articulate what the data is proving.

But what about the companies where management felt the analytics *were* working? In these businesses, 63% of executives responded to a Harvard Business Review survey saying they could see a positive impact on their Key Performance Indicators when they implemented predictive analytics. As a result, HBR concluded these companies were better at identifying problem areas and making the necessary adjustments to fix it.

When interviewed for a Harvard Business Review Report, Lori Bieda, BMO's head of the Analytics Centre of Excellence, Personal and Business Bank said, "Insights are the easy part, but you have to take rapid action on them to gain competitive advantage."

Instead of just deciding analytics don't work—or don't work—for your company, take the time to have employees trained to use the software. The time and money is well spent to get the most out of this 21st century innovation.

Sources
xl

Chapter 16
Finding the Right Employees in a Changing Economy

"I choose a lazy person to do a hard job. Because a lazy person will find an easy way to do it."
– **Bill Gates**
Founder, Microsoft

Recent changes to tax and regulatory policies in the U.S. have shifted the economy into great shape. According to an August 2018 survey from the National Federation of Independent Business (NFIB), small business owners have never been more optimistic about what the future holds. And as businesses grow, so do the number of job openings.

In fact, an all-time high of 7 million job positions were waiting to be filled by potential employees, reported a July 2018 JOLTS survey. A record number of job openings is due in part to a rising job quit rate, which rose to a 17-year high of 2.4 percent that same month. This means that almost 4 million Americans had recently quit their jobs, many of whom were looking for new employment opportunities.

It seems that an increasing number of firms are looking to hire qualified candidates and, from looking at the rising job-quit rate, an increasing number of Americans are looking for new employment.

So why did the NFIB report that 89% of small business owners who attempted to hire found no or few qualified candidates? Why are firms struggling to make ends meet in the recruitment process?

In a separate survey from the NFIB, one-quarter of business owners identified their single biggest challenge to be hiring qualified workers.

Making consistently effective hiring decisions can be a daunting challenge for many corporate recruiters. The process of recruiting and selecting qualified candidates is more of an art than a scientific process. What can be a scientific process—and what can power an efficient, systematic approach to selection—is employing assessment tests, otherwise known as workforce analytics.

In most organizations, candidate selection is a continuous, multi-step process, although the steps can vary with the type of company and level of the job. A typical approach to a systematic selection procedure is shown below.

Organizations use several different means to obtain information about applicants—everything from resumes to interviews to employment tests. Although employment tests are just one part of a holistic application process, they are crucial in accurately predicting a candidate's performance in the workplace. Effective pre-employment assessments can measure, among other things, an applicant's cognitive skills, personality traits, aptitude for learning.

Types of Employment Tests

Employment assessments and tests can be classified in different ways. Generally, they are viewed as measuring either a candidate's aptitude or achievement.

Cognitive Ability Tests

Cognitive Ability tests measure mental capabilities such as general intelligence, verbal fluency, numerical ability, and reasoning ability. A variety of tests, whether administered through a computer or on paper, measure cognitive abilities. Examples include The Predictive Index System®, the General Aptitude Test Battery (GATB), and the Wonderlic Cognitive Ability Test.

PRO: Cognitive ability tests are best indicative of a candidate's general intelligence, as opposed to specialized areas of intelligence such as reading comprehension and spatial relations. Highly proficient general mental abilities have been shown to be great predictors of performance, as well as career success and job satisfaction.

CON: Sometimes these tests can be viewed as unfair—by both manager and candidates.

Personality Assessments

Unlike cognitive ability tests, personality tests focus less on a candidate's mental capacity and more on personal characteristics such as extroversion, agreeableness, and openness to experience. This type of awareness can be useful when assessing candidates for managerial roles and job positions that require a high degree of communication with other people.

PRO: Testing for a candidate's personality traits can be indicative of how well that person will fit into the company culture and can be used as part of a career development program or for enhancing productivity in a team-based environment.

CON: Personality tests can be problematic if they inadvertently discriminate against individuals who would otherwise perform effectively.

Physical Ability Tests

In addition to learning about a job candidate's cognitive and behavioural abilities, employers may need to assess a person's physical abilities. This is especially true for jobs that are conducive to physically demanding work environments and potentially dangerous jobs such as the roles of firefighters, police officers, and truck drivers.

Physical abilities such as strength and endurance tend to be good predictors not only of performance on the job but also of the ability to minimize injury. It should be noted, however, that physical ability tests are not the same as medical examinations—which are often excluded from the hiring process due to potential challenges of privacy invasion and discrimination.

PRO: For certain professions, a physical ability test may be the best indicator of job performance, particularly in professions where the difference between meeting and failing the physical standard could result in injury or loss of life.

CON: Determining a standard to which candidates must adhere can be difficult. The standard must be derived from some sort of basis and should not aim to discriminate against certain groups, such as a particular gender, for example.

Job Sample Tests
Job or work sample tests require the applicant to perform tasks that are a part of the work required on the job. These assessments are constructed from a carefully developed outline and must be reflective of the job's major functions.

These tests are usually implemented for jobs that require secretarial or clerical skills—although there are many exceptions to the mean. Examples include a map-reading test for traffic control officers, a lathe test for machine operators, a complex coordination test for pilots, a group discussion test for supervisors, and a judgment and decision-making test for administrators.

PRO: These assessments are a great way for candidates to prove, beyond certainty, their ability to perform well on the job.

CON: Work sample tests must be comprised of job functions that are directly related to what is explicitly stated in the job description. Otherwise, implementing this employee test is a waste of time and resources.

Finding the right employees can be difficult, especially in the 21st century economy with its fierce talent-competition. Luckily, hiring tools can help companies cut through the noise and single out candidates who will not only show up to work with a smile on their face but also contribute to the culture and growth of the company as well.

Sources
xli xlii xliii xliv

Chapter 17
Staying Competitive During the Holiday Hiring Season

"When things get busy, it is often too easy to fall behind in the hiring process, leaving current staff swamped and unhappy."

As companies gear up for the holiday season, they are often in need of a larger workforce to handle increased production. But competition for candidates during the holidays can be stiff. In the hectic pace of the holidays, how do you ensure that your company is attracting the best candidates possible?

As the holiday season ramps up, life at work will only get increasingly stressful. That is why it is important to start searching for seasonal help early. Hiring early provides a safeguard against being overworked or understaffed later on.

When things get busy, it is often too easy to fall behind in the hiring process, leaving current staff swamped and unhappy. Hiring early is also important because it provides time to adequately train new employees in order to maximize efficiency.

The hiring process begins by releasing your job listing to the public. Job listing search engines such as Indeed receive up to 230,000 new jobs every month. That's a lot of competition.

To ensure that your posting differentiates itself among the sea of available employment opportunities, you can pay to sponsor your job listing on platforms such as Monster and Indeed. This relatively inexpensive process far increases the likelihood that the perfect candidate will click your job listing, among the thousands of others.

Regardless of who you are, everybody has a life outside of work. The holiday season puts a special emphasis on building and maintaining relationships with friends and family.

For your job posting to be as attractive as possible to potential candidates, allow for flexible work schedules where possible. This does not mean you have to let employees choose their own hours. For example, flexible work schedules can be as simple as excusing workers who show up five minutes late to their shift due to traffic or harsh weather conditions.

Beyond accommodating for different work schedules, employers can also offer a benefits package. A typical benefits package in Canada might include a small amount of Life Insurance, Accidental Death and Disablement Insurance, Extended Health, Dental, and Employee Assistance Programs.

Although this can seem expensive, benefit packages for temporary workers can do wonders in the long run. Gord Donas, a former human resources consultant at Morneau Sobeco, says "benefits are quite simply a requirement when it comes to attracting and retaining staff."

Finally, a positive work environment is important because it is conducive to employee satisfaction and productivity. Keep in mind that seasonal workers may return to the business next season, turn into customers, or be great referral sources for the future. Building a positive relationship between the worker and the business can be beneficial in the long run.

Next time a big holiday comes around, instead of dreading the process, see the hiring spree as an opportunity to build cultural champions and brand ambassadors.

Sources
xlv

Chapter 18
The Power of Employee Engagement

"Company culture is all that matters."
— Gary Vaynerchuck,
CEO, VaynerMedia

The same way a puck bounces around the ice rink, the term "employee engagement" floats around the workplace. But does it mean anything— or is it just another empty buzzword? By the testimony of Craig Richardson, chief executive of global fabric manufacturer Canadian General-Tower, it is not.

Defined as the extent to which employees feel passion and commitment to their jobs by exerting discretionary effort into their work, employee engagement could be integral to driving employee recruitment and retention.

The Economic Case for Employee Engagement

Recruiting and retaining human capital can be one of a company's most expensive investments. In fact, the Society for Human Resource Management estimates that the average cost-per-hire in 2016 was $4,425. Although not an insignificant cost, unlocking the full potential within employees can be integral to establishing a competitive edge in the market.

In terms of retention, the average cost-per-hire is dwarfed by the average cost of turnover—anywhere from $8,000 to $213,000 depending on employee salary level, according to SHRM. Given the financial benefits of investing in long-term employees, employee engagement and satisfaction are crucial to ensure that turnover costs are minimized within the company.

Beyond the direct costs, there are many intangible costs associated with losing dispassionate employees. Common examples include loss of productivity and loss of engagement spreading to other workers.

Developing new recruits to a level of satisfactory efficiency can take months or even years as new hires acclimate to an unfamiliar office space. Additionally, workers who witness high turnover rates in the office could also disengage from their work; office morale is also likely to dip. An engaged employee, by contrast, is likely to provide a surplus of value by going above and beyond what is required of their role.

Best Practices to Improve Employee Engagement

Reducing employee turnover begins with a strong foundation that supports long-term talent retention. By building an organizational culture of recognition for exceptional performance and innovative ideas, managers and executives and lay the brickwork for this base.

Another idea is to instill the idea that recruitment is a long-term investment and not an immediate cost. By doing so, managers can assess how they can nurture their employees so that their investments appreciate. They should consider what tools can be provided to maximize employee development and contribution. This empowers employees—especially when they are autonomously allowed to make decisions.

Encouraging the sharing of creative ideas can sometimes be all it takes to engage an employee. By allowing employees the freedom to innovate, morale can be boosted, and retention rates can rise favourably.

To add the cherry on top, the careful examination and integration of performance appraisal system can be beneficial. This motivates employees to actively partake in creating performance milestones that track their growth and development. Throughout the year, managers should request updates on employee performance and provide recognition when appropriate.

Try to think of the last time you were completely engaged in what you were doing. Who made you feel like that? What did they do? How can you re-create that in your business?

Sources
xlvi xlvii xlviii

Chapter 19
4 Benefits of Behavioural Interviewing

"Behaviour drives people, people drive business."
- Anonymous

Behavioural questions. Nearly every interview has them—situational behavioural questions that ask candidates to draw upon their past experiences are becoming increasingly popular. They have become part of the interview process standard in a wide variety of industries, from corporate banking to sales to management consulting.

Regardless of the nature of employment, most recruiters want to know if the candidate being interviewed will be able to perform well in the workplace—if they are able to add value to the company. Performing "well" can constitute an amalgam of qualities, everything from having the necessary technical background to being able to assimilate into the company culture. It is this latter quality into which behavioural questions can provide superior insight.

Behavioural questions that require prospective job candidates to articulate their experience in particular situations allow the interviewer to get the most out of the interview process. These sorts of questions glean the most pertinent information out of the interviewee, allowing employers to obtain a better overall view of what a candidate would be like in the workplace. Additionally, open-ended behavioural questions such as "tell me about a time you overcame objectives to close a difficult sale" create an opportunity for detailed follow-up questions, making the flow of the interview a little more natural.

This is about being able to "walk the talk." Anybody can say on their resume that they have superior leadership skills or that they are seasoned problem solvers. In fact, according to a 2017 employment screening benchmark report by 85% of employers caught applicants falsely altering their resumes or applications.

Behavioural questions help to partly circumvent this issue by pushing job candidates to go beyond their resume. Providing solid, concrete examples of past experiences in the interview room is more difficult to fabricate than simply writing a falsification on a resume.

For example, when interviewing candidates for an office management role, asking a situational question about their experience with simultaneously juggling multiple tasks allows recruiters to see exactly what that candidate has accomplished in his or her previous roles.

Traditional interview questions are common to nearly every interview prep guide online. Anybody who does a little bit of preparation before the interview will be able to answer questions such as "what are your strengths and weaknesses" or "tell me about yourself." Behavioural questions, however, are easily customizable to the employment position at hand. Since they can be so specific, it is more difficult for prospective candidates to prepare for them, allowing the interviewer to see past the surface of a well-polished and rehearsed interviewee.

An often overlooked, but crucial part of being able to perform well in the workplace, is the ability to work well within the structure of the company culture. Sometimes candidates will have great skills and work histories but will not be the best match for a specific job.

Behavioural interviews allow recruiters to gain a deeper insight into the personality and the drivers of the individual. If a potential applicant is team-oriented and has relevant previous experience, but the position they are applying for requires high levels of autonomy, they are not the right fit for that role. The only way to extract this kind of information is by employing behavioural questions in the interview process.

Sometimes the most qualified applicants are the worst interviewers. When their nerves get hauled into overdrive, suitable candidates might not represent themselves in the best light. Behavioural interview questions can make candidates less nervous by making the flow of conversation more natural. Since the focus of these sorts of questions is akin to telling a story in a normal conversation, candidates will feel more comfortable, allowing them to rid their feelings of anxiety or nervousness.

Behavioural questions, when integrated properly, can maximize the value recruiters receive from the interview process, providing a backup and reassurance that the candidate will carry out their responsibility, and be an asset to the team.

Sources
xlix

Chapter 20
The Toronto Raptors and Talent Over Resume

"I think if you're going to be a little bit innovative or risk taking, sometimes you're going to be wrong and it's going to look bad. I understand that. If they don't work, I'll stand in front of you guys, take the heat."

- Nick Nurse
Head Coach, Toronto Raptors

Nick Nurse was brought in as the head coach of the Toronto Raptors at a time when no one thought Toronto even needed a new one. Dwayne Casey had just been named the NBA's Coach of the Year, an award that generally guarantees your employment for a while.

One day after the awards show, Raptors president Masai Ujiri sent Casey packing, bringing then assistant coach Nick Nurse into the spotlight as the Raptor's next head coach.

This was a bit of a shock to Raptor's fans across Canada. Nurse had what is often referred to as the skinny resume—not flashy or filled out. In Nurse's case, this was especially true. He hadn't played at a big-name NCAA school (University of Northern Iowa), never played in the NBA, and his coaching career took him mostly to Europe, the G-League, and the Summer League.

By contrast, the man coaching against Nurse in the 2019 NBA finals, Steve Kerr, played for the University of Arizona, played for Team USA at the FIBA World Championships, played for three NBA teams over a 20-year career, was an NBA analyst, and then worked in the front office of the Phoenix Suns before moving to Golden State and coaching the team to three NBA championships in four years.

So, how was Nurse so successful? He is a natural fit for his job. He has the right mix of assertiveness, patience, and drive to coach in the NBA.

To prove this, you need only look at his childhood basketball career. As a kid, playing in a tournament final with only seconds to go, the young Nurse took over the huddle from the head coach, drew up a play, and the team won the game.

Not the best player on the court, Nurse's teammates say he had paid more attention to fundamentals than anyone else, something that would become instrumental to his success with the Raptors.

Nurse was eventually the youngest coach in the United States collegiate program, at just 23-years-old. However, saying Nurse was an under-the-radar-coach was still an understatement.

It took a while for him to break into the NBA. Nurse's former players call him a genius for his ability to use unconventional methods to score. He had his players run a "box and one" defence style in the 2019 NBA finals against superstar Stephen Curry. The play, generally only used by children's basketball teams, took Curry by surprise, helping the Raptors to contain Golden State's biggest shooter. This unconventional playing style took the Raptors to their first ever NBA Championship win and solidified Nurse's status as a top NBA coach.

How does this connect to business?

It would have been very easy for Masai Ujiri to hire another experienced NBA coach or to have just kept Dwayne Casey. No one would have said anything. Keeping the NBA Coach of the Year is generally supported.

However, sometimes no matter how strong a resume looks it is more important to look at someone's behaviour and their non-work traits. How do they fit into your job model? For example, is this person impatient to cross the street but the job requires composure? Do they pay attention to the small details in their emails to you for a developer role? These subtle hints can help you to understand who someone truly is at their core.

Sources

l li lii liii

Chapter 21
Managing Employee Engagement: Google and The World of Workplace Analytics

"We want Google to be the third-half of your brain." –
Sergey Brin
Co-founder, Google

Engagement. It's the dial you can't see. It's on no dashboard, and yet, it is an aspect of every single action that takes place in a company. In one survey of over 500 executives by The Predictive Index, 71% said employee engagement was important to them but only 24% said they believed their employees were engaged.

Engagement is the driver of a company. Take Google, a 'Best Places to Work' winner every year. Google is touted as a change maker, a leader in workplace analytics, and it's the prestigious logo to have on your LinkedIn. "I work at Google" has become the stuff of legend.

It's held this way because the company engages its employees, makes them feel valuable, and treats them like assets, not machines.

Google also uses data to add to its workplace quality. To quote an article about Google from the Culture Summit, "Google's entire approach to business—including how the company drives engagement—revolves around data."

So how does data allow you to manage employee engagement?

The Google Method

Google uses what it calls "gDNA" to figure out a person at their core. This allows the company to hire the right person for the job, someone who can be given the flexibility to work, has the drive for the job, and will continue to perform down the road. By finding the right fit, Google ensures it will have an engaged employee—someone whose output and inner drive for the role are both high.

Once they have this, all of the added bonuses of working for Google— the free haircuts, food, and napping areas—are all bonuses that make employees feel valued. The right fit makes them happy at their core, the perks make them happy in their heads. All around, you have an engaged employee.

What are the pitfalls of *not* having an engaged employee? According to a Gallup study, 34% of the employee's salary. For someone making $60,000 a year, that could mean an incredible $20,400 each fiscal period.

To avoid this, managers can employ empirical and analytical methods to ensure their employees are right for the job (engaged in their core) and given the right perks (engaged in their head).

The first step is to ensure the work you are asking someone to do is identifiably meaningful. Sometimes this means laying out for the employee how their work will benefit the team. A simple task such as lead generation can have a huge impact on a company but can seem like a minuscule task if framed poorly. To measure whether your employees feel like they are getting meaningful work, listen in to the office chatter. Mike Zani, CEO of The Predictive Index, has talked about this struggle from the employee's view saying, "If your salary is in the normative range yet you're constantly saying you're not paid enough, that's a clear sign of disengagement."

As well, create an environment where people want to work. This may seem stereotypical of a technology start-up but the concept does truly work for employees. Give employees comfy spaces to work, ease up on stay at your desk policies, and provide access to drinks and caffeine that make the work process more enjoyable. This will be even more important as Generation Z enters the workforce. This age group values workplace culture over pay and these little perks are a great way to peak their engagement.

Think of the last time you knew you were in your element. It felt great, right? By using analytical systems employers are ensuring employees feel this way every day.

Happy core, happy head. A mix for engagement.

Sources
liv lv lvi lvii lviii lix lx lxi

Part 3: Creating Generational Champions

Chapter 22
Hiring and Retaining the Millennial Workforce

"The Millennial Generation will entirely recast the image of youth from down-beat and alienated to upbeat and engaged – with potentially seismic consequences for America."

– Neil Howe and William Strauss
Authors, *Millennials Rising*

Millennials, those born between 1983 and 1995, are always a hot topic of discussion in the human resources management community. How is this new generation of workers different from the last? How can we leverage the expertise of this hyper-connected group of workers to our company's advantage? How do Millennials survive off nothing but avocado toast and tall non-fat lattes with caramel drizzle?

According to a study from the Pew Research Center, more than one-in-three labour force participants are Millennials, making them the largest generation in the workforce. That number will grow to 60% by 2020, a fact corroborated by the LinkedIn Global Recruiting Trends 2018 report.

The potential challenge is there's ample room for miscommunication between generations. Gallup reports that Millennial turnover in the U.S. alone costs organizations $30.5 billion annually. It is therefore imperative that recruiters and managers understand the distinct needs of Millennial workers, so as to avoid the consequences of an unsatisfied and unproductive employee base.

How can we work with them?

Stress the Importance of Their Work

A simple stroll into any gathering of young professionals will reveal that this younger generation places a high emphasis on leaving an impact. Millennials want to know that their work is valued and that it can generate tangible results. Beyond being fed a list of duties and responsibilities, Millennials need to know why their work is important and how it fits into the grand scheme of things. When recruiting for younger candidates, ensure that they understand the significance of their role to the larger strategy of the company.

Avoid Corporate Jargon

From huge neon billboards to inconspicuous product placement, advertisements are everywhere these days. And nobody has experienced it more than the Millennials. When searching for companies, Millennial prospects tend to veer away from workplaces described in dated and superfluous language. Instead, they are attracted to companies that speak to them in a succinct, relatable way. Stay clear of buzzwords, corporate jargon, and anything else that can be deemed as divisive.

Be a Mentor, Not a Boss

About 44% of young professionals expect to leave their current employers in the next two years and 65% reported personal development as the most influential factor of their current job.

Young workers want to know whether it is possible to advance their careers within the company and how they can continually build their skills for larger roles in the future. Ensure managers sit down with employees and plan a clear roadmap of where they see themselves in five or ten years. This will lead to greater success retaining new hires.

Give Praise Where Praise is Due

Nobody likes working when they feel unappreciated. Recognize, share, and reward exceptional work whenever possible. One idea is to implement a milestone rewards program, allowing employees to work toward a goal, instead of aimlessly clocking in and out of the office.

Support Flexible Schedules (If Possible)

As employers and industries are becoming increasingly flexible, so are employee schedules. The traditional 9-to-5 is a corporate structure of the past. Work-life balance is an important criterion for Millennials in the job search and professions that allow for flexible hours, telecommuting opportunities, and extra vacation time are likely to see higher employee retention.

It's Not Just Money They're After

Everybody can offer a competitive salary. Sometimes it is the employee perks and the company culture that can sway a potential job prospect one way or the other. Small benefits such as casual dress codes, family-friendly policies, and health club memberships can go a long way.

Be Open to New Communication Styles

Fifty years ago, nobody could have imagined that one of the most powerful computing devices of the last century would be able to fit in a pant pocket. A testimony to the progress of technology and connectivity, cell phones have opened a plethora of alternative communication styles.

From face-to-face to over-the-phone to messaging apps, Millennials communicate with each other in a variety of ways. Understanding how young employees prefer to communicate and trying to accommodate that preference can be beneficial in the long run.

More Feedback, Fewer Problems

In a hyper-competitive job market, employees are itching to stand out. One way they can do this is by honing and mastering their workplace skills. To help facilitate this need, managers can provide real-time feedback to employees, instead of the traditional and overly formal performance review. Even a simple weekly 10-minute meeting can foster an open and honest relationship between the manager and the employee.

Help Yourself by Helping the Community

Many Millennials are passionate about global challenges and enjoy being involved with their local community. A recent survey of Millennials from the SHRM revealed that 47% of young employees volunteered on their own for a cause or non-profit in the previous month, 94% enjoyed using their skills to benefit a cause, and 57% want more company-wide service days. Holding regular fundraisers or community outreach events can boost employee morale and heighten their sense of purpose in the workplace.

Embrace their Tech Skills

Millennials grew up in the middle of a technological revolution, implying that their aptitude for technology is a cut above the rest. By embracing technology in the recruiting and employee development processes, managers can ensure their employee base will consist of the best and the brightest.

Sources
lxii lxiii lxiv

Chapter 23
Hiring and Retaining Generation Z

"The people who work for you aren't building a company for you, they are building it for themselves - they are the center of their own universe. Just because you are the CEO, doesn't mean they are coming to work every day to make you happy. They want to be happy and it's your job to keep them that way."

- Ben Lerer
CEO, Thrillist

Born after 1996, Generation Z is slowly becoming a part of the workforce, the purchasing audience, and the global leadership community. With over 2.52 billion young adults, Generation Z is already bigger than its parents' generation. Still young during the last recession, Generation Z has been a part of 94 consecutive months of job creation. Their eyes are wide to the possibilities of the workforce, watching companies like Uber, Facebook, and Snapchat rise from nothing to billion-dollar-plus valuations.

Like their older counterparts, the Millennials, Generation Z cares more about what they do then how much they make, meaning employers can't rely on pay increases alone to retain top talent. Here are the best ways managers can effectively harness the power of Generation Z.

Support Social Causes

This is a big part of keeping Generation Z on your team. Growing up with social media, bad business has been in front of these young adults their whole lives. On the flip side, they have also seen the growth of companies like TOMS, whose marketing campaigns relied on their social work. Generation Z wants to work with companies that align with their social conscience. About 10-20% of Generation Z are willing to take a pay cut to work for something they care about.

Flexibility if possible

Generation Z are digital nomads. With low barriers to entry, the internet has made it possible to gain side sources of income from online businesses that cost nothing to start. About 4.8 million Americans already call themselves digital nomads. Generation Z sees the internet as a way to create better work from anywhere. They don't see the office as the place they have to be. If your business can swing it, let them work where they best unleash their innovation and creativity.

Grow them as a person

Generation Z wants to see their career path and know they can grow in their field. They know that they are competing every second of the day and want any advantage they can get. The best way to foster this is to mentor them. Set aside a few minutes a week to meet with an employee over coffee, field their questions, offer your take. As social creatures, this time for them is much more valuable than it may seem.

Create a company culture

Company culture matters. A side-effect of social media is an increase in Generation Z's social drive. They want to be friends with their co-workers, they want to collaborate. Rainmaker Thinking found that the top "need" in a company for Generation Z was the culture. Last place? Pay.

Pay less, spend the savings on coffee machines, company trips, and upgrading the office. It will pay off.

Curiosity drives them

Generation Z chooses their fields because they interest them. About 83% said they chose a career path because they were very interested in the field. By comparison, only 39% said that potential compensation made them choose. Let Generation Z be curious, explore interests and new technologies. If you can afford it, give employees time and money to work on personal projects that relate to the company. That's how Gmail was created.

They will be entrepreneurial

Another side-effect of social media? Generation Z knows they are small in comparison to the greater world. A big driver of what they do is based on a desire to have an impact. The path they see to this is through entrepreneurship. About three-quarters of Generation Z respondents indicated they wanted to own a business. Why? They believe this is the path to having an impact. Great managers will allow Generation Z workers to follow this entrepreneurial drive and its underlying impact goals to build their company. Let them start offshoots, extra projects, and derive new business they can own.

Sources
lxv lxvi lxvii

Chapter 24
Corporate Social Responsibility:
A Must with Gen Z.

"The only corporate social responsibility a company has is to maximize its profits."
– Milton Friedman
Nobel Prize-winning economist

At one time, corporate social responsibility (CSR) was used to make a company stand out. Connecting themselves to causes their consumers' valued was a great way to build brand trust, distinguish themselves from competitors, and drive marketing campaigns that made people think about the company. However, the concept dates back further than one may guess.

In the 1800s, Andrew Carnegie wrote about the almost moral obligation of CSR in *The Gospel of Wealth*, writing:

"Thus, is the problem of Rich and Poor to be solved. The laws of accumulation will be left free; the laws of distribution free. Individualism will continue, but the millionaire will be but a trustee for the poor; entrusted for a season with a great part of the increased wealth of the community but administering it for the community far better than it could or would have done for itself. The best minds will thus have reached a stage in the development of the race which it is clearly seen that there is no mode of disposing of surplus wealth creditable to thoughtful and earnest men into whose hands it flows save by using it year by year for the general good."

In 1943, Robert Johnson, founder of Johnston & Johnston, made CSR a part of his companies' credo:

"We are responsible to the communities in which we live and work and to the world community as well. We must help people be healthier by supporting better access and care in more places around the world. We must be good citizens — support good works and charities, better health and education, and bear our fair share of taxes. We must maintain in good order the property we are privileged to use, protecting the environment and natural resources."

Although both men should be applauded for their early insights into the social role of the company, that ideology is no longer innovative—it's the norm.

For Generation Z consumers, CSR is not an option for a company. Thanks in part to the immediacy of social networks, they have seen mistakes in real time (sometimes uncut) and can stay up to date on every developing misstep a company makes, with a forum to let them know. This information allows these young consumers to make active decisions about what brands to trust and support.

In one survey, 76% of Generation Z buyers said they have purchased, or would consider purchasing, from a company that supports social causes to support those efforts. Possibly more important for the average business owner, 67% of that same group said they have avoided purchasing from, or would consider avoiding purchasing from, a company that did not stand for what they believed in.

This isn't a generation to take lightly anymore either. Generation Z makes up 40% of all active consumers and has an annual spend of $200 billion globally.

CSR is even penetrating the classroom. Investment students are now being taught to evaluate companies based on their ESG—or environmental, social, and governance performance. Just over one-quarter (26%) of all professionally managed assets in the United states are invested sustainably, according to the Global Sustainable Investing Alliance in 2018, up from just 18% four years earlier.

As Generation Z becomes influencers in the global workplace, marketplace, and securities markets, companies will need to place greater emphasis on their CSR and sustainable practices.

Even small and medium enterprises can make impacts with their CSR. By focusing on their immediate region, these SMEs can support smaller initiatives with a smaller budget and still give back to their local community. These local projects often require less capital, and can allow team members to volunteer with each other—a great team and culture-building exercise.

Without this type of forward-thinking, businesses open themselves to the risk of being labeled a profit-hungry enterprise. A death-label for some businesses.

To execute CSR plans, companies need to align their social-conscious behaviour with their strategic communication plan, an often-overlooked aspect of a business' PR.

Business is full of buzz words. Big data. Contextual marketing. Corporate synergy. Growth hacking. Hyperlocal.

Most of these terms have real value for those looking to grow in the ever-changing business landscape—even if they are overused. For example, big data truly is, and will continue to be, a tool that businesses can use to grasp and contextualize their clients and positioning in the marketplace. Hyperlocal advertising is an incredibly effective way to tailor your marketing efforts by a specific area's interest (for example, think about making your marketing materials reflect the local hockey team's colours).

However, these words get a bad rap from blog posts and articles that start with *"5 tips to grow big with…,"* *"How to increase your followers with…"* and best of all *"The secret tip to…"*

Strategic communication is stereotyped as one of these words, but in this marketplace, it may well have the biggest impact of all. Strategic communication's definition can be boiled down to one question: "How do we as a business *purposefully* craft a message to the public that is consistent with our brand and our strategic goals?"

In the days of cellphones and social media, no business is safe from a bad PR move, but even more importantly, safe from a *well-intentioned* PR move that is perceived poorly. Think Pepsi's "Global message of unity, peace and understanding" campaign. The intention was there but the execution was a PR disaster.

We asked a graduate student in a communications program to explain the role of strategic communications within organizations.

Why is strategic communications important?

For a number of reasons. First, it prepares an organization to respond to and manage issues by having the company think really hard, well in advance of a crisis, about its organizational goals and values and let that guide its response to future challenges. This means your business is always scanning the environment, monitoring and analyzing issues that may affect it, so you are ready for any threats. Second, strategic communication builds relationships with stakeholders because part of what drives the process is your own values and concern for your reputation. You will seek ways to foster those relationships in the short, medium and long-term. Finally, strategic communications involves the entire organization. It's not about issuing press releases. It's thinking about who you are and what you represent and embedding that in all communications – whether that's internally with staff and shareholders or externally with the public, politicians or others.

How can poor strategic communication affect businesses?

You've heard the saying "the left hand doesn't know what the right hand is doing?" That's an organization with poor strategic communication. It reacts in the moment in knee-jerk fashion. Consider the United Airlines incident when it physically removed a passenger from a flight and social media blew up. With a stronger strategic communications plan, the airline would have analyzed all of the 'what ifs' around overbooked flights, social media, and the potential for public backlash. Advice from a communications specialist would probably have benefited the airline by pointing out the potential for reputational damage when asking security guards to physically remove a passenger. A well thought out communications strategy would have provided a guide for the organization at every step in the process.

What can businesses do to encompass strategic communication with their public relations?

This should be flipped the other way around! Public relations is a *component* of the strategic communications plan. It is just one communication pathway for a company. That said, corporate communications should be driving the strategic communications plan. With input from senior leaders, managers, staff, shareholders, etc., communications professionals can offer a big-picture vision of potential threats and issues and offer guidance on how best to navigate them using the communications tools available.

Sources
lxviii lxix lxx lxxi

Part 4: The Interviews

Chapter 25
An Interview with A Gen-X Blockchain & Internet of Things (IoT) Business Leader

As a professional in the Generation X demographic working in a field that is still very new and rapidly developing, how do you stay up to date and current?

I have always had a passion for learning and science specifically. As a graduate student in neuroscience, I was able to use technology (early machine learning) to validate my research and model behaviour before testing on animals. It changed my view that technology was not just a simple tool but an enabler of transformation in my field.

As my newfound excitement for technology grew, I joined the tech world in 2000 as the internet was going through the tech bubble and saw firsthand the fusion of internet and technology. It is then I decided to always look at and expand my knowledge of cutting and leading-edge technology. It became a passion. Fast forward to today and I am still pushing myself to learn and become an advocate for technology I believe can change the way we work and live.

In the last five years I have worked with in-memory databases, Artificial Intelligence, IoT, Blockchain and am ramping up now on Quantum Computing. To stay current in these fields, I actively use LinkedIn (make contacts, join groups, discussions, take courses), take advantage of free online learning, education from my employer, attend conferences and Mars seminars, TED talks, podcasts, articles and finally talk with organizations and people to see how these technologies impact their business (and how they will transform them).

As a member of Generation X, what is it like working closely with Millennials and Generation Z?

When Millennials first joined the organizations I worked for, I noticed a difference in how we worked, how we learned and how we interacted. I would research and look for answers on my own before reaching out to other SMEs, and in my experience, Millennials would reach out and ask for coaching and help sooner.

Generation Z is quite interesting. They are very adept at using technology to their advantage and tend to gravitate towards emerging technology (Blockchain has quite a few budding entrepreneurs). With this generation I see more gamification of the workplace compared to X or Millennials. Very knowledgeable and able to find whatever information they need quickly and independently.

There is an interesting dynamic where my generation favours building relationships and communicating in-person, the Z generation is very much online, remote, competitive and the Millennials somewhere in the middle.

What do you see as the future role of data in the workplace?

Data is king. Data is the most important asset an organization has. To make decisions in a quickly changing world, organizations need to use the available data to adapt, pivot, innovate and attract/retain the right talent. I have seen, over the last 20 years, talented people mismatched to roles that do not challenge them, excite them or utilize their specific skill-set and expertise, thereby lowering overall productivity.

Matching the talent to the roles will drive productivity, to do this we need data. Currently there is a tech skillset shortage and that shortage is going to grow as digitization and automation expand exponentially. Driving an organizational culture of continuous learning and providing education to existing employees will start to shrink the skillset gap. To ensure the education is tailored to the right people with a current skillset to fill future roles, data needs to be current and relevant.

What do you see as the future of the workplace for your kids, and the rest of Generation Z?

I see a very different workplace compared to 20+ years ago. Technology is moving at an accelerated rate thereby constantly changing the workplace. Generation Z and my kids will need to learn to adapt, continuously upgrade their knowledge and skills, able to predict and pivot to changing roles/jobs and not be afraid to take on challenges. The future is very much a changing and transforming landscape that will permeate every aspect of our life.

Move to a skill-based economy, gamification, remote access to our organization and customers, holographic meetings, automation, 5G, processing of Quantum computing, robotics and AI will be mainstay in everyday roles. Many of today's jobs will no longer exist (travel agents, cashiers, librarians, postal couriers, bank tellers, textile workers, the print industry, sports referees and umpires, manufacturing, long haul drivers, taxi/Uber drivers, etc.) and future roles/jobs have yet to be created (chief productivity officer, drone traffic controller, quantum data analyst, sustainable building regulator, human-robot mediator, waste engineer, etc.).

The main skillset that will be an absolute requirement in majority of future jobs will be logic and coding (which we are woefully unprepared for with today's educational system).

Chapter 25

An Interview with a Gen-X Videographer at a Major Canadian News Network

As someone working in an industry that is constantly changing, how do you keep up?

It is sort of a two-fold answer. First, I am fortunate enough to work for an employer that places a high-importance on training. Anytime something new comes out, it is accompanied by voluntary hands-on training. Second, I tend to go to the younger videographers at work, some of our newest hires, who tend to have a better grasp on the latest technology that is hitting the market. I ask them about new gear, what they are using, etc. As someone with no social media profile, I don't see the new releases online, and thus, I either have to search for it myself or ask them.

You work in an job where every day is different. How do you come to work and perform at a high-level when you may not even know what you will be asked to do?

I have a strong set of fundamental skills that I've developed over the years, and I have to adapt them to each scenario I encounter in a day. It could be a lighting problem, technical malfunction, weather issue, etc., but the problem-solving skills are all the same. You rely on your core skills. To be a high-performer in a constantly-changing job, you need to focus on building your fundamental strengths and then adapting them to the job situation. Adapting on the job is crucial. When you have confidence in your fundamental skills, you can adapt to a changing situation and continue to perform at a high level when you're thrown a curve ball.

You work with different people every day, mixing and matching team members to get a certain story done. How do you build a high-performing culture when you never know who you are going to be working with?

When working with different people each day, we generally let each other lead in our strong areas. If I'm working with someone with a strong lighting background, we agree that he or she will lead there, and I'll facilitate the camera set-up. It's about understanding each other's strengths and how to use them. If you're smart about it, you'll observe those who have a strength in an area you don't in order to work on the constantly developing the skillset I mentioned earlier. When you're working with a peer, keep the ego at the door. You have to recognize that each person on your team is a professional, just like you. At the end of the day, we all have one common goal.

Chapter 28
Conclusions and the Future

You'll notice a lot of interesting things as you walk into a meeting at the company of the future.

First, you may not even walk to the meeting. As connection technologies like Zoom Meeting improve, the entire interaction may take place online. If it is a face-to-face meeting however, it is likely the meeting will take place at the local Starbucks. Because of the low barriers to entry for new tech companies, many top-performing businesses are comprised of 'digital nomads'. These are people you see working on their laptops at your local coffee shop, able to run their company from anywhere with an internet connection.

Now, if the company does have an actual office, you will notice some differences as soon as you walk in. The office will mildly resemble a living room. This isn't just to show off a 'relaxed' workspace; the beanbag chairs and bar-style tables will be in use almost the entire day. A big part of what the (mainly) Millennial and Generation Z workforce at this company loves is that their employer promotes open communication and collaboration. Teamwork at this company isn't something executives and managers have to drill into the employees, it comes naturally to them.

You will also feel a happier atmosphere. The HR team uses hiring analytics to make sure everyone they hire is a natural fit for the job; it doesn't matter if the team is stressed, they love it. The stress fits their personality. They'll view it as a project, not a chore.

You'll shake your head a bit. In the corner will be the $10,000 coffee machine, smoothie bar, fully stocked fridge, and a group of people standing around talking and sipping on beverages. Listen in to their conversation and you'll hear them talking about something that is obviously not at all related to their job. "A waste of productive time," you'll think, "Taking advantage of the amenities of the office and slacking off." Listen in a bit further and you'll hear that the project is actually an idea an employee had at home one evening, and is now recruiting others in the business to work on with them. This project is what the employees work on during their break. The company will nurture the idea, provide resources, and eventually, incorporate the project into the core business plan. No more chat about the hockey game or new movies; these employees are engaged, and will use every ounce of their day, break or not.

When you finally arrive at the manager's office, you'll ask them why everyone seems to get along, or at least seems to be able to work with each other's blind spots. The manager will tell you that they have behavioural profiles on each employee and that the teams actively use the data for self-awareness and team projects.

You'll leave with only one thought. "Was that even a business?" There was no manager watching over individual employees, half of the team was working remotely, everyone seemed genuinely engaged in their work, and even when there were events that can cause friction—say, team projects—everyone seemed to know their blind spots.

Data drives analytics. Analytics drives culture. Culture drives results.

The Journey to Cultural Championship:

Creating a passionate, driven, and high-performing team

Do you want to try behavioural analytics at your company?

Visit www.predictivesuccess.com or call (905) 430-9788 for five free behavioural assessments for you next hire.

References

[i] https://resources.predictiveindex.com/wp-content/uploads/2019/03/CEO_preferences_disrupting_consulting.pdf

ii Kaplan, Soren. "The Business Consulting Industry Is Booming, and It's About to Be Disrupted." Inc.com. September 11, 2017. Accessed June 21, 2019. https://www.inc.com/soren-kaplan/the-business-consulting-industry-is-booming-and-it.html.

iii Beck, Barry LibertMegan. "AI May Soon Replace Even the Most Elite Consultants." Harvard Business Review. July 24, 2017. Accessed June 21, 2019. https://hbr.org/2017/07/ai-may-soon-replace-even-the-most-elite-consultants.

iv "Artificial Intelligence in Cars Powers an AI Revolution in the Auto Industry." Built In. Accessed July 03, 2019. https://builtin.com/artificial-intelligence/artificial-intelligence-automotive-industry.

v Ray, Linda. "Employee Turnover Statistics in Restaurants." Small Business - Chron.com. October 26, 2016. Accessed June 21, 2019. https://smallbusiness.chron.com/employee-turnover-statistics-restaurants-16744.html.

vi Premack, Rachel. "The Fast Food Industry Is Facing a Growing Crisis." Business Insider. May 01, 2018. Accessed June 21, 2019. https://www.businessinsider.com/mcdonalds-taco-bell-fast-food-turnover-technology-2018-4.

vii Lachapelle, Justine. "The Restaurant Turnover Rate Is Astronomical. Here's Why (And How to Fix It)." ChefHero. October 04, 2018. Accessed June 21, 2019. https://www.chefhero.com/blog/restaurant-turnover-rate.

viii "Canada Ranks 4th Globally for Highest Employee Turnover." Canadian HR Reporter. Accessed June 21, 2019. https://www.hrreporter.com/culture-and-engagement/36271-canada-ranks-4th-globally-for-highest-employee-turnover/.

ix O'Donnell, J.T. "85 Percent of Job Applicants Lie on Resumes. Here's How to Spot a Dishonest Candidate." Inc.com. August 15, 2017. Accessed June 21, 2019. https://www.inc.com/jt-odonnell/staggering-85-of-job-applicants-lying-on-resumes-.html.

x Lucas, Suzanne. "When No Resumes Makes for Better Hiring." Inc.com. January 11, 2016. Accessed June 21, 2019. https://www.inc.com/suzanne-lucas/when-no-resumes-makes-for-better-hiring.html.
xi "Identifying and Closing Skills Gaps." The Predictive Index. May 30, 2019. Accessed June 21, 2019. https://www.predictiveindex.com/blog/identifying-and-closing-skills-gaps/.

xii "Employers View Resumes for Fewer than 11 Seconds." Workopolis Blog. June 25, 2015. Accessed June 21, 2019. https://careers.workopolis.com/advice/employers-view-resumes-for-fewer-than-11-seconds/.

xiii Posted by: Admin. "11 Social Media Recruiting Statistics to Make You Rethink Your Current Strategies." Profiles. September 20, 2017. Accessed June 21, 2019. https://www.careerprofiles.com/blog/hiring-innovative-talent/11-social-media-recruiting-statistics-to-make-you-rethink-your-current-strategies/.

xiv "Millennials Are Largest Generation in the U.S. Labor Force." Pew Research Center. Accessed June 21, 2019. https://www.pewresearch.org/fact-tank/2018/04/11/Millennials-largest-generation-us-labor-force/.

xv McDaniel, Scott, and Steve Beger. "MarketingSherpa Consumer Purchase Preference Survey: Demographics of Customer Reasons to Follow Brands' Social Accounts." MarketingSherpa. January 07, 2016. Accessed June 21, 2019. https://www.marketingsherpa.com/article/chart/demographics-why-customer-follow-brands-social-media.

xvi "3 Ways to Be Constantly Recruiting Star Talent Through Social Media." Monster.ca. May 16, 2019. Accessed June 21, 2019. https://hiring.monster.ca/employer-resources/recruiting-strategies/attracting-job-candidates/recruit-talent-through-social-media-ca/.

xvii "Reports and Insights | Global Trust in Advertising and Brand Messages." Nielsen. Accessed June 21, 2019. https://www.nielsen.com/us/en/insights/reports/2012/global-trust-in-advertising-and-brand-messages.html.

xviii "Blog #1: The History and Roots of Predictive Analytics." SalesChoice. Accessed July 03, 2019. https://www.saleschoice.com/the-history-and-roots-of-predictive-analytics/.

xix Bureau of Labor Statistics. "THE EMPLOYMENT SITUATION — MAY 2019." News release, June 7, 2019. Accessed July 3, 2019. https://www.bls.gov/news.release/pdf/empsit.pdf?mod=article_inline.

xxhttps://www150.statcan.gc.ca/n1/en/pub/75-004-m/75-004-m2018001-eng.pdf?st=biMg3vp3

xxi ibid.

xxii CareerBuilder. "Nearly Three in Four Employers Affected by a Bad Hire, According to a Recent CareerBuilder Survey." PR Newswire: Press Release Distribution, Targeting, Monitoring and Marketing. June 26, 2018. Accessed June 21, 2019. https://www.prnewswire.com/news-releases/nearly-three-in-four-employers-affected-by-a-bad-hire-according-to-a-recent-careerbuilder-survey-300567056.html.

xxiii O'Donnell, J.T. "85 Percent of Job Applicants Lie on Resumes. Here's How to Spot a Dishonest Candidate." Inc.com. August 15, 2017. Accessed June 21, 2019. https://www.inc.com/jt-odonnell/staggering-85-of-job-applicants-lying-on-resumes-.html

xxiv "Canada Unemployment Rate." Canada Unemployment Rate | 2019 | Data | Chart | Calendar | Forecast | News. Accessed July 03, 2019. https://tradingeconomics.com/canada/unemployment-rate

xxv Statistics Canada. "Labour Force Survey, April 2019." The Daily - . May 10, 2019. Accessed July 03, 2019. https://www150.statcan.gc.ca/n1/daily-quotidien/190510/dq190510a-eng.htm.

xxvi www.predictivesuccess.com

xxvii https://www.shrm.org/hr-today/trends-and-forecasting/research-and-surveys/Documents/2017-Talent-Acquisition-Benchmarking.pdf

xxviii Google Search. Accessed July 08, 2019. https://www.google.com/search?q=social media marketing to generation z&oq=social media marketing to generation z&aqs=chrome..69i57j69i60l3j35i39j69i59.6956j0j7&sourceid=chrome&ie=UTF-8.

xxix Williams, Kaylene & Page, Robert. (2011). Marketing to the Generations. Journal of Behavioral Studies in Business. 3. 37-52

xxx Toms. "Gift of Shoes: TOMS® Giving." Gift of Shoes | TOMS® Giving. Accessed July 08, 2019. https://www.toms.ca/what-we-give-shoes.

xxxi "When Was the First Computer Invented?" Computer Hope. November 13, 2018. Accessed June 21, 2019. http://www.computerhope.com/issues/ch000984.htm.

xxxii "A Brief History of Predictive Analytics - Part 1." After Inc. December 28, 2018. Accessed July 08, 2019. http://www.afterinc.com/brief-history-predictive-analytics-part-1/.

xxxiii "Re:Work - Great Managers Still Matter: The Evolution of Google's Project Oxygen." Google. Accessed July 08, 2019. https://rework.withgoogle.com/blog/the-evolution-of-project-oxygen/.

xxxiv "People Management Study Results." The Predictive Index. Accessed July 08, 2019. https://www.predictiveindex.com/management-survey-2018/.

xxxv "What Gen Z Wants From Work." HRExecutive.com. October 01, 2018. Accessed June 21, 2019. http://hrexecutive.com/what-gen-z-wants-from-work/.

xxxvi Gassam, Janice. "How Generation Z Will Impact Your Workplace." Forbes. January 02, 2019. Accessed June 21, 2019. https://www.forbes.com/sites/janicegassam/2018/12/26/how-the-newest-generation-generation-z-will-impact-your-workplace/#408f05dc2af6.

xxxvii "In China's Tech Industry, the 72-hour Work Week, Dubbed the 996, Has Bosses Singing Its Praises." The Globe and Mail. April 17, 2019. Accessed July 08, 2019. https://www.theglobeandmail.com/business/technology/article-in-chinas-tech-industry-the-72-hour-work-week-dubbed-the-996-has/.

xxxviii Ryerson, Lia. "What an Average Work Day Looks like in 18 Countries around the World." INSIDER. May 15, 2018. Accessed July 08, 2019. https://www.insider.com/office-work-day-around-the-world-2018-5#a-whopping-two-hour-lunch-break-falls-in-the-middle-of-the-work-day-in-both-italy-and-china-7.

xxxviii Howard, Ryan. "We Gave Our Employees Fridays Off Paid and Now We Have an Amazing Team." Entrepreneur. July 15, 2016. Accessed July 08, 2019. https://www.entrepreneur.com/article/278823.

xxxix "5 Traits That Make Passionate Workers Drivers of Success." Refresh Leadership. July 24, 2013. Accessed June 24, 2019. http://www.refreshleadership.com/index.php/2013/07/5-traits-passionate-workers-drivers-success/.

xl "Uncovering the Keys to Becoming Truly Analytics-Driven." Harvard Business Review. May 08, 2018. Accessed June 24, 2019. https://hbr.org/sponsored/2018/05/uncovering-the-keys-to-becoming-truly-analytics-driven.

xli "May 2019 Report: Small Business Optimism Index." NFIB. Accessed June 24, 2019. https://www.nfib.com/surveys/small-business-economic-trends/.

xlii "Job Openings and Labor Turnover Summary." U.S. Bureau of Labor Statistics. June 10, 2019. Accessed June 24, 2019. https://www.bls.gov/news.release/jolts.nr0.htm.

xliii Bloomberg.com. Accessed June 24, 2019. https://www.bloomberg.com/news/articles/2018-09-11/job-openings-in-u-s-increased-in-july-to-record-6-94-million.

xliv "Small Business Optimism Shatters Record Previously Set 35 Years Ago." NFIB. September 11, 2018. Accessed June 24, 2019. https://www.nfib.com/content/press-release/economy/small-business-optimism-shatters-record-previously-set-35-years-ago/.

xlv Driver, Saige. "6 Tips for Hiring Seasonal Help." Business News Daily. September 22, 2017. Accessed June 24, 2019. https://www.businessnewsdaily.com/6641-seasonal-hiring-tips.html.

xlvi "Employee Engagement Isn't Just a Buzzword – It's a Competitive Advantage." The Globe and Mail. January 02, 2019. Accessed June 24, 2019. https://www.theglobeandmail.com/business/commentary/article-employee-engagement-isnt-just-a-buzzword-its-a-competitive/.

xlvii https://www.shrm.org/hr-today/trends-and-forecasting/research-and-surveys/Documents/2017-Talent-Acquisition-Benchmarking.pdf

xlviii   https://www.americanprogress.org/wp-content/uploads/2012/11/CostofTurnover.pdf

xlix O'Donnell, J.T. "85 Percent of Job Applicants Lie on Resumes. Here's How to Spot a Dishonest Candidate." Inc.com. August 15, 2017. Accessed June 24, 2019. https://www.inc.com/jt-odonnell/staggering-85-of-job-applicants-lying-on-resumes-.html.

l "How Small-town Iowa Boy Nick Nurse Led the Toronto Raptors to NBA History | CBC News." CBCnews. June 14, 2019. Accessed June 20, 2019. https://www.cbc.ca/news/world/nba-finals-nick-nurse-1.5174697.

li "Maybe Not the Raptors First Choice, but No Doubt Now Nurse the Best One." Sportsnet.ca. Accessed June 20, 2019. https://www.sportsnet.ca/basketball/nba/maybe-not-raptors-first-choice-no-doubt-now-nurse-best-one/.

lii Patton, Jessica. "Nick Nurse's In-game Adjustments Help Lead Toronto Raptors to NBA Championship." Global News. June 14, 2019. Accessed June 20, 2019. https://global-news.ca/news/5375494/nick-nurse-toronto-raptors-nba-championship/.

liii "Steve Kerr." Wikipedia. June 17, 2019. Accessed June 20, 2019. https://en.wikipedia.org/wiki/Steve_Kerr.

lv "7 Employee Engagement Best Practices from the HR Experts at Google." Culture Summit. March 14, 2018. Accessed July 02, 2019. https://www.culturesummit.co/articles/employee-engagement-best-practices/.

lvi "How to Calculate the Cost of Employee Disengagement." LinkedIn Learning. Accessed July 02, 2019. https://learning.linkedin.com/blog/engaging-your-workforce/how-to-calculate-the-cost-of-employee-disengagement.

lvii "Global Talent Trends 2019." Business Solutions on LinkedIn. Accessed July 02, 2019.   https://business.linkedin.com/talent-solutions/recruiting-tips/2018-global-recruiting-trends.

lviii Adkins, Amy. "Millennials: The Job-Hopping Generation." Gallup.com. April 20, 2019. Accessed July 02, 2019. https://www.gallup.com/workplace/236474/Millennials-job-hopping-generation.aspx.

lix "Deloitte Global Millennial Survey 2019." Deloitte. May 24, 2019. Accessed July 02, 2019.   https://www2.deloitte.com/global/en/pages/about-deloitte/articles/Millennialsurvey.html.

lx "Maximizing Millennials: The Who, How, and Why of Managing Gen Y." Maximizing Millennials: The Who, How, and Why of Managing Gen Y - Blog | MBA@UNC. June 24, 2013. Accessed July 02, 2019. https://onlinemba.unc.edu/blog/geny-in-the-workplace/.

lxi Gurchiek, Kathy. "Millennial's Desire to Do Good Defines Workplace Culture." SHRM. April 10, 2018. Accessed July 02, 2019. https://www.shrm.org/Re-sourcesAndTools/hr-topics/behavioral-competencies/global-and-cultural-effectiveness/Pages/Millennial-Impact.aspx#sthash.Nz3kssWR.I9cn6ZXB.dpuf.

lxiii "Employee Engagement and Productivity." The Predictive Index. Accessed July 02, 2019. https://www.predictiveindex.com/how-we-help/engage-employees/.

lxiv Fry, Richard, and Richard Fry. "Millennials Are Largest Generation in the U.S. La-bor Force." Pew Research Center. April 11, 2018. Accessed July 02, 2019. http://www.pewresearch.org/fact-tank/2018/04/11/Millennials-largest-generation-us-labor-force.

lxv Gassam, Janice. "How Generation Z Will Impact Your Workplace." Forbes. January 02, 2019. Accessed July 02, 2019. https://www.forbes.com/sites/janicegas-sam/2018/12/26/how-the-newest-generation-generation-z-will-impact-your-workplace/#408f05dc2af6.

lxvii "What Gen Z Wants From Work." HRExecutive.com. October 01, 2018. Accessed July 02, 2019. http://hrexecutive.com/what-gen-z-wants-from-work/.

lxviii Hessekiel, David. "Engaging Gen Z In Your Social Impact Efforts." Forbes. June 28, 2018. Accessed June 20, 2019. https://www.forbes.com/sites/da-vidhessekiel/2018/06/26/engaging-gen-z-in-your-social-impact-efforts/#1428be364995

lxix https://www.forbes.com/sites/biancamillercole/2019/03/11/retailers-listen-up-6-ways-to-speak-to-gen-z/#18fd461fbfd0

lxx Advanced Solutions International, Inc. Corporate Social Responsibility: A Brief His-tory. Accessed June 20, 2019. https://www.accprof.org/ACCP/ACCP/About_the_Field/Blogs/Blog_Pages/Corporate-Social-Responsibility-Brief-History.aspx.

lxxi "Our Credo." Content Lab - U.S. December 14, 2018. Accessed June 20, 2019. https://www.jnj.com/credo/.

Made in the USA
Middletown, DE
19 August 2019